# Developing Global New Products
## Challenges to U.S. Competitiveness

# Research for Business Decisions, No. 94

Richard N. Farmer, Series Editor

Professor of International Business
Indiana University

## Other Titles in This Series

# Developing Global New Products
## Challenges to U.S. Competitiveness

by
Dean G. Van Nest

UMI Research Press
Ann Arbor, Michigan

Produced and distributed by
UMI Research Press
an imprint of
University Microfilms, Inc.
Ann Arbor, Michigan 48106


Library of Congress Cataloging in Publication Data

**Van Nest, Dean G. (Dean Gillette), 1923-**
Developing global new products.

(Research for business decisions ; no. 94)
Revision of thesis (Ph.D.)—Pace University, 1985.
Bibliography: p.
Includes index.
1. New products.   2. New products—Management.
I. Title.   II. Series.
HD69.N4V36   1987        658.5'75'0973            87-5844
ISBN 0-8357-1793-3 (alk. paper)

*To my wife, Diana, and my children,*
*Dean Jr., Ross, and Kathleen*

# Contents

# Acknowledgments

The development of this book has been far from a one-man effort and represents the time, patience, and knowledge of many individuals. First, I wish to thank the people who originally launched me into the controversial world of global marketing: Janet Wolff, my business associate for many years; Dean Van Nest, Jr., a confirmed global marketer; and my many multinational clients. Their hours of discussing, arguing, and laying out the pros and cons spurred me on.

Second, I want to thank Dr. Warren J. Keegan for his guidance. His extensive experience as teacher and well-known writer in the international field was truly invaluable. I am equally grateful to members of the Pace University faculty for their advice, support, and counsel: Dr. Verne Atwater, Dr. Elayn Bernay, Dr. Oscar Nestor, and Dr. Robert Vambury. I would also like to acknowledge the help received from Dr. Gad Selig, another leading authority in the international field.

Third, I offer a collective thank you to the many executives who participated in the study. I am particularly grateful to the special panel of presidents who contributed their up-front guidance on the research: George Goebeler, Robert Phillips, William Jackson, Ed Shutt, and J. Tylee Wilson.

# 1

# New Product Development and Emerging World Markets

## The Change in New Product Development

There has been a profound change in one of the most essential areas of American business—new product development. This is a change unnoticed by many U.S. companies. It is a change some companies recognize yet ignore. This change, however, could seriously affect U.S. growth and impede its worldwide competitiveness.

The United States has always been proud of the innovative ability that drives new product development. From the days of Thomas Edison and Henry Ford, there has been a swashbuckling, restless quality about U.S. inventiveness. Whether it be the richness and depth of discovery of a Bell Laboratories, the venturesomeness of a 3M, or the determination of a Lee Iacocca—we have forged ahead. Whether it was the Horatio Alger-like success of Apple Computer or the precision and professionalism of a major Procter and Gamble roll-out—there has been a momentum and excitement to new products on the U.S. scene. Whether it be the intuition of a Wang or the high-tech prowess of an IBM—we have always displayed a unique blend of innovation and creativity.

But now a new change has emerged which U.S. business must deal with—the necessity to look at new product development in world terms. When a Swiss businessperson dreams of a new product, the odds are very high that it will be in terms of export; the size of the market in Switzerland makes that a necessity. When the Dutch think of a new innovation, interest in international sales is apt to be automatic. Because of their limited national market size, the British, Japanese, French, and West Germans are all born with an "export or die" philosophy.

Our large U.S. market, however, has tended to lull American business into an incredibly local focus. We see only the profitable market in front of us. New product development in the U.S. has been concerned with consumer research in Seattle, market tests in Peoria, product usage studies in New Orleans, and West Coast rollouts. We are provincial when it comes to being entrepreneurial.

We have a national boundary phobia about new product development. This obsession with self is dangerously stifling for the long run. This same obsession has also meant that fewer than 15% of all U.S. companies even engage in any type of international trade and that fewer than 300 U.S. companies account for 85% of all U.S. exports.

Like it or not this national boundary phobia must change. The convergence of cultures, the speed at which new products can be copied worldwide, and the global viewpoint of major world competitors who are making substantial competitive inroads even in our own country, make this local focus hopelessly out of date. We have rapidly approached the hour when new product development on a national boundary basis is as outmoded as the slide rule or last year's microchip. More and more we are competing in a living, breathing global economy which has found its way very successfully to our retail shelves and dealerships. Our national boundary phobia must be eliminated and we must think of new product development in an entirely new and more challenging way.

Some of our leading multinational companies have already reacted to this change. Procter and Gamble, for example, has put new emphasis on finding faster ways to roll out new products internationally once they have proven successful in one country or area. Gillette and Colgate have looked for more effective ways to coordinate new product development among subsidiaries, thus avoiding duplication of effort and maximizing the speed of international introductions. IBM has led the way in centralizing this function by creating a new product development group whose responsibility is to coordinate new products on a world basis.

One question, however, remains: How will the majority of U.S. companies respond to this change?

**The Importance of Successful Innovation**

Innovation and new product development are more than ever the keys to the future success of U.S. companies worldwide. As Peter Drucker has said of the turbulent times ahead:

> We need a strategy that will enable existing businesses first to identify the opportunities for innovation and then to give effective leadership in such innovation. . . . In the period ahead, the old-fashioned companies will only succeed—or even survive—if they can set up innovation as a major distinct business.[1]

Vital as innovation and new product development may be, however, this activity cannot be truly successful if most U.S. companies continue to ignore a whole new dimension for the future—the needs of world markets. Overlooking this world viewpoint will seriously impede U.S. companies' multinational competitiveness and limit the United States as a future worldwide marketer.

There is a substantial gap between new product development as practiced in this country today and what it would be if world markets and a "globalization" strategy were taken into account. My premise is:

1. The "globalization of markets" concept is being utilized by increasing numbers of U.S.-based multinational consumer goods companies on *existing* products.
2. Globalization is *not* being adopted by these companies for *new* product expansion.
3. To implement global new product development, these U.S. companies would require *major* changes in their current new product programs— changes in philosophy, methodology, and organization.

With *established* products, an increasing number of companies are putting emphasis on world markets and are trying a more universal, integrated, globalized approach. Yet in the most critical area of company performance— new product development—many U.S. companies are still operating as if established products and new products were on completely different tracks. These companies fail to consider the global implications of new products. They fail to realize that the development of products for single-home markets may be as wrong now as the development of *local* brands instead of *national* brands in the early 1900s.

For most U.S. companies, new product programs are conducted without regard to the rest of the world. New product development is carried out as though the possible worldwide sale of these products is an unrelated second phase which may or may not occur in the distant future. Rather than looking up-front at world markets as the real potential for new innovation, the focus is home-country oriented. An even worse situation is the multinational company that allows its new product development program to be fragmented worldwide—permitting each country to pursue new product development in isolation. The unfortunate fact is that today, in most U.S. companies, unconscious blinders limit this important function to national boundaries.

**The Need to Know More**

I first became aware of this need for change in new product philosophy through personal business experience with a series of U.S. multinational companies. In recent years these companies had one common characteristic—they were all adopting a more integrated, worldwide marketing strategy.

The top management of these companies had accepted two important premises. First, that U.S. companies were losing their competitiveness worldwide to foreign-based multinational companies which operated with a more universal, worldwide marketing approach. Second, that increasing convergence of cultures and consumer needs was making it possible to operate with a more efficient, universal marketing strategy.

The "pains" involved in adapting to this new globalized strategy were many: problems of acceptance within the organization; problems of headquarters versus local authority; problems of staffing with the proper skill and talent; and problems of communication and implementation.

In spite of these difficulties, an increasing number of U.S. multinational companies have moved in this direction over the last few years. In the fall of 1984, a Harris poll of 600 marketing executives showed that 46 percent felt their company would move even more into global marketing.[2]

This movement has brought with it considerable controversy as to the wisdom and practicality of such an approach. The controversy was polarized even more in the spring of 1983 by Theodore Levitt's landmark *Harvard Business Review* article "The Globalization of Markets."[3] Today the pros and cons of Levitt's article continue to be argued in marketing circles.

Perhaps one of the most controversial areas has been global new product development. There are those who believe we are moving into a period in which new product development for world markets will be an absolute necessity. There are those who feel that new product development for introduction into a single country is the only practical strategy.

With the exception of isolated reports in the press, little information has been assembled on any quantitative basis to determine what U.S.-based multinational companies think about global new product development, or what, if anything, is actually being done about the concept.

The globalization movement has tended to involve vocal comment from scholars, advertising agencies, and new product consultation services. Many company executives have tended to remain silent for reasons of confidentiality or, perhaps, until management adopted a policy on the issue.

Because it has become increasingly obvious that there is a great need for more factual information, a quantitative study on new product development practices among U.S.-based multinational companies was conducted by the author in 1985. This survey covers high-level executives of 137 leading U.S. companies who sell consumer goods and services internationally. One hundred percent of the responses obtained are from the level of vice president or above—one third being chief executive officers (CEO) and presidents. Seventy percent of the respondents have been actively involved with new products for more than 10 years.

The major objective of the study was a description and analysis of the new product development process in these companies. Secondary objectives included identification of whether these companies have a global or local focus in their new product programs and whether the premise regarding national boundary new product development is correct. Emphasis was placed on the following critical questions:

*Philosophy and Strategy.* What was the geographic focus of their new product development program? Was there a current recognition of the need for global acceptance of new products then being developed? Was globalization a part of the long-term strategic plan for the company?

*Organization and Structure.* How was the company's new product development program currently organized? Was it a corporate or divisional function? Were international marketing personnel a regular part of the structure?

*Methodology and Process.* What was the new product development process currently being followed? Was globalization incorporated in any way into the planning, development or evaluation process?

To attack the most difficult area of global new product development, the study concentrated on consumer goods and services companies rather than those companies involved with high-tech, agricultural, or industrial products. Many have believed that it is one thing to globalize high-tech or industrial products but quite another to standardize approaches on highly culturally sensitive consumer goods and services.

In the worldwide competitive arena, U.S. consumer goods companies have faced a particularly hard task. First, many U.S. consumer goods companies have, in numerous world areas, fallen behind the stronger foreign-controlled multinationals such as Rowntree Mackintosh, Heineken, Sony, Henkel, BSN, Beecham, Rickitt & Coleman, Nestlé, and Unilever. Second, U.S. consumer goods companies have not been strong in export. Consumer goods represent only eight percent of all U.S. exports which are overwhelmingly industrial, high-tech, and agricultural. In absolute dollars, U.S. consumer goods imports are four times greater than consumer goods exports—evidence of stiff competition from foreign-based multinationals.[4]

Exploring the global new product development issue in terms of consumer goods has, therefore, been believed to be the acid test of the global strategy.

## Definitions

In the international field in particular, confusion often exists as to what is meant by certain terms. For example, to many the term "global marketing" means having a worldwide viewpoint; to others the words mean marketing with a universal approach worldwide.

So that we can discuss the situation with a common understanding, let us define the following terms as they are used in this book:

*Existing products* are those products that are already present in the product mix of the company involved. It is recognized that these could be new products in some overseas areas when exported by the company. For the purpose of this discussion, however, they are not new products to the company involved.

*New products* are those products new to the company involved, whether it be a line extension or a complete innovation. In this sense the product refers to the total entity—the brand name, the package, the physical product, etc.; or for a service, the brand name and service involved. In this discussion, we will use the terms product and brand interchangeably referring to the total entity being sold by the company.

*Consumer products* are those products and services sold primarily to individual consumers on a mass, frequent purchase basis—foods, drugs, toiletries, cigarettes, beverages, soaps. This would not include high-tech, industrial, or agricultural products.

*National brands* are those products/brands sold in a single country or home market. When national brands are extended overseas using a highly standardized home-country marketing mix, this is an ethnocentric approach to marketing worldwide.

*Multinational brands* are products/brands sold in many countries using an individualized marketing mix for each country. These brands are often the result of what is called the multidomestic or polycentric approach to marketing worldwide.

*Global or world brands* are products/brands sold in many countries using a more standardized, universal marketing mix for each country. These brands are often the result of what is called a geocentric approach to marketing worldwide.

*Globalization* refers to the concept of standardizing the marketing mix for a product worldwide as currently popularized by Theodore Levitt and his globalization of markets concept. To globalize would mean to utilize a universal marketing mix for selling the product worldwide based on an integrated, interactive, worldwide marketing approach.

*Global marketing* refers to marketing global or world brands with a highly universal, standardized marketing mix.

*New product development* refers to the process used by the company to plan for, develop, and evaluate a new product prior to its introduction as part of the company's product mix.

*Global new product development* refers to the process used by the company to plan for, develop, and evaluate a new product as a global brand for eventual introduction into several markets. As a global brand, the marketing mix for this product would be highly universal and standardized.

# 2

# The "Globalization of Markets" Controversy

In his landmark article "The Globalization of Markets," Theodore Levitt crystallized what many multinational experts have been thinking for some time: "Companies must learn to operate as if the world were one large market—ignoring superficial regional and national differences."[1]

The literature has been filled with articles echoing Levitt's cry. In the halls of both multinational and large U.S. companies, globalization has been a highly controversial subject.

The basic thinking behind the concept is well explained in Levitt's original article:

> The globalization of markets is at hand. With that, the multinational commercial world nears its end and so does the multinational corporation. . . . The multinational and the global corporation operates in a number of countries and adjusts its products and practices in each—at high relative costs. The global corporation operates with resolute constancy—at low relative costs—as if the entire world (or major regions of it) were a single entity; it sells the same things in the same way everywhere. . . . Which strategy is better is not a matter of opinion but of necessity. . . .
>
> The modern global corporation contrasts powerfully with the aging multinational corporation. Instead of adapting to superficial and even entrenched differences within and between nations, it will seek sensibly to force suitable standardized products and practices on the entire globe. They are exactly what the world will take, if they come also with low prices, high quality, and blessed reliability. . . . Companies that do not adapt to the new global realities will become victims of those that do.[2]

Levitt not only crystallized the thinking on world brands and global marketing, he also advanced his concept at a most appropriate time. It was the moment in U.S. history when full attention was being given to finding new ways for improving the U.S. competitiveness worldwide.

## The Need to Improve U.S. Competitiveness Worldwide

Bruce Scott and George Lodge put considerable focus on the issue of U.S. worldwide competitiveness in their book *U.S. Competitiveness in the World*

*Economy*.[3] Robert Reich and Ira Magaziner also emphasized this problem in *Minding America's Business*.[4] All these articulate writers stressed that a new approach to international marketing was critical for the future position of the United States.

The general line of reasoning used by these writers follows this scenerio. First, U.S. companies, and particularly multinationals, must greatly improve their international competitiveness if they are to survive. The U.S. faces severe worldwide competition from other developed countries—principally Japan, Germany, France, and the European Community. Since 1950, the U.S. share of world trade has dropped from 20 to 11 percent. Since 1971, the U.S. trade balance has turned negative reaching an estimated record high in 1986 of $174 billion.[5] Furthermore, because the U.S. represents only 20 percent of today's world market, the future growth for most U.S. companies is very dependent on international expansion.

Second, U.S. companies have been slow to enter either Third World or developed countries because of the perceived risks involved. At the same time, world competitors have built economies of scale into their businesses by developing business in the Third World countries as well as the developed countries. This leverage, combined with the U.S. tendency to leave foreign competitors unchallenged in their own markets, has given our competitors a very strong base from which to compete.

Third, U.S. companies have tended to take short-term, fast profit positions in dealing with international business. They have relied too heavily on licensing and short-term export sales. They have been reluctant to engage in long-term joint ventures and direct investment.

Fourth, U.S. companies have fallen behind worldwide competition because of their very home-oriented, ethnocentric approach to marketing. This lack of any genuine world viewpoint has often involved unrealistic pricing unrelated to the local market situation. It has meant, in many cases, the sale of lower quality goods with a lower price/value relationship than products offered by world competitors. It has meant, too, inadequate development of the right product/communication strategies for global markets.

Scott, Lodge, Reich, Magaziner, and Levitt all reach at least one common conclusion. For the future success of U.S. companies, it will be essential to adapt a new approach to international business. It will also be vital to utilize the most competent talent the company has available to accomplish this mission.

With this as a backdrop, why, then, has Levitt's seemingly farsighted approach brought about so much controversy?

## Universality—The Major Source of Disagreement

*Advertising Age* reported: "The controversy grows. . . . [T]he most provocative marketing and advertising issue today is globalization, . . . described by some as a corporate ego trip." Philip Kotler, one of the country's leading marketing educators, has taken an openly opposing view proclaiming that "Ted is *wrong* on this one!"[6] After hearing Levitt's Four A's speech, many in the audience reportedly said they "wouldn't touch his concept with a ten-foot pole."[7] One of the country's largest agencies called global marketing "a dangerous siren song for naive marketers."[8]

The basic controversy over Levitt's globalization theory centers around his focus on *universality* and *standardization*. In an age when the emphasis has been on the "marketing concept," catering to individual needs/wants and unending segmentation, the Levitt concept, to many, seems out of step. Levitt states emphatically "that people all over the world have the same tastes and desires . . . that people are remarkably alike regarding love, hate, fear, greed, envy, joy, patriotism, pornography, material comforts, mysticism and the role of food in their lives." "At *issue,*" continues *Advertising Age,* "is Mr. Levitt's latest theory . . . [that] the world is becoming a common marketplace in which people—no matter where they live—desire the same products and life styles. Global companies must forget idiosyncratic differences between countries and cultures and instead concentrate on satisfying universal drives."[9]

The very meaning of global marketing has recently undergone a change. What once meant "marketing on a worldwide basis" has become, according to Levitt's definition, "marketing with a universal, standardized approach worldwide."

In a recent round-table discussion with marketing leaders, Levitt reinforced his definition:

> [H]istorically, the multinational corporation has operated precisely as its name suggests— that is, it operates pretty much everywhere. . . . [I]t functions in ways that are presumed to be appropriate to those places, those nations, given the preference structures of the people there, the channels of distribution, the legal constraints, the various other institutions and the histories of the cultures. That is what multinationality means—or, multi-domestic.
>
> The global corporation, by contrast, will think of the world becoming—as, indeed, I believe it is—increasingly more homogeneous; where, although there may be important national borders and national interests that define a nation, commercially the nations are defined really more by the common things that bind them together, rather than the uncommon or historic things that separate them.[10]

Levitt then expands on the idea of convergence. He attributes this convergence to "proletarianization" (widespread accessibility) of communication, transportation, and travel. His followers have expanded on the concept of convergence even further. For example, Robert Jordon advances the idea of convergence in demographics, culture, and habits.

Jordon advocates that in the modern industrial world, the convergence of such demographic trends as aging populations, falling birth rates, and increased female employment are extremely significant to world markets. He points out (see table 1) that the effects in terms of household composition have been the

## Table 1.  Examples of Convergence

### HIGHER LIVING STANDARDS

GROWTH IN REAL PERSONAL CONSUMPTION 1970–82

| | |
|---|---|
| US | +42% |
| UK | +26% |
| FRANCE | +60% |
| GERMANY | +34% |
| JAPAN | +65% |

SOURCE: HENLEY CENTRE

### MORE WORKING WOMEN

% CHANGE 1970–1980

| | WORKING POPULATION | WORKING WOMEN |
|---|---|---|
| US | +24.4 | +37.6 |
| FRANCE | +7.7 | +17.3 |
| UK | +4.5 | +15.1 |
| GERMANY | −1.6 | +3.5 |

SOURCE: EUROSTAT

### DECLINE OF THE FAMILY UNIT

AVERAGE NUMBER OF PERSONS PER HOUSEHOLD

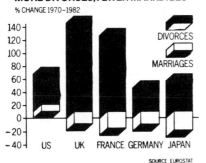

■ 1960  ◻ 1981

| | 1960 | 1981 |
|---|---|---|
| US | 3.33 | 2.73 |
| UK | 3.10 | 2.65 |
| FRANCE | 3.15 | 2.76 |
| GERMANY | 2.88 | 2.46 |
| JAPAN | 4.10 | 3.30 |

SOURCE: HENLEY CENTRE

### FEWER NEW CONSUMERS (000s)

| | 1983 | 2000 |
|---|---|---|
| Age Segment | 15–19 | 15–19 |
| FRANCE | 4,225 | 4,102 |
| US | 19,845 | 18,888 |
| UK | 4,482 | 3,709 |
| JAPAN | 8,933 | 8,726 |

SOURCE: HENLEY CENTRE

### GROWTH OF SELF-SERVICE RETAILING

AS A % OF TOTAL GROCERY SALES  1976 ◻  1980 ■

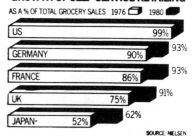

| | 1976 | 1980 |
|---|---|---|
| US | 99% | |
| GERMANY | 90% | 93% |
| FRANCE | 86% | 93% |
| UK | 75% | 91% |
| JAPAN· | 52% | 62% |

SOURCE: NIELSEN

### MORE DIVORCES, FEWER MARRIAGES

% CHANGE 1970–1982

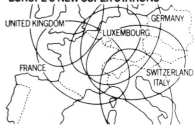

DIVORCES
MARRIAGES

US  UK  FRANCE  GERMANY  JAPAN

SOURCE: EUROSTAT

### EUROPE'S NEW SUPER STATIONS

UNITED KINGDOM  GERMANY  LUXEMBOURG  FRANCE  SWITZERLAND  ITALY

Source: Saatchi & Saatchi Worldwide, London, England.

universal decline of the nuclear family with fewer children per household and a declining proportion of households which conform to the two-adult-two-children pattern. Jordon also points out the *universality* of the increase in working women as well as the growth in living standards/personal consumption over the last 12 years.[11]

Jordon attributes culture convergence largely to communication—television and motion pictures being the major factors. He advances the idea, too, that "most observers believe cultural convergence will proceed at an accelerated rate through the next decade particularly with the development of high powered broadcast TV satellites throughout Europe which will for the first time allow viewers access to international television without the barrier of language."[12] The convergence in demographics and culture, Jordon points out, leads even to convergence in habits. For example, as Saatchi and Saatchi show, "the widespread erosion of the traditional family unit and the increase in working women has led to the decline of formal meal taking and the corresponding increase in the use of 'instant' or convenience foods, snack-pot meals, and the use of fast food restaurants."[13]

The Global Media Commission of the International Advertising Association is another group advocating global marketing because of convergence. Their emphasis is communication convergence—largely television, cable TV and potential satellite television services. As the commission explains in its foreword to *Global Marketing* report:

> It's the breakthrough marketing tool of the '80s, and it's going to transform the advertising and television industries in the decades to come.
>
> Global marketing—a simple name for a complex new approach to worldwide business. Some experts think the concept spells the end of multinational corporations as they know them today. Global marketing means selling inexpensive, high-quality, reliable products. Selling the same products in all the nations of the world. And selling them with highly unified marketing techniques. No longer will there be a different advertising campaign for each country or each language of the world. Increasingly, products and their marketing support systems will be truly global.
>
> Why now? Why should business practices that always have been theoretically possible seem so urgently in need of development?
>
> Because of television, the undisputed heavy weight champion of advertising.
>
> Many countries around the world severely limit television advertising, even ban it altogether. Those barriers are falling, their foundations washed away by the irresistible tide of technology—video cassette recorders, cable television and a wide variety of potential satellite television services.
>
> World-class products being sold by uniform advertising campaigns on commercial television around the world—those are the elements discussed in detail in *Global Marketing—From Now to the Twenty-first Century.*[14]

The overall reception to Levitt's theory of universality has been widely divergent. While high-tech companies such as IBM or Apple have been working in this direction for some time, consumer goods marketers have been much slower to act. Even among companies in the same product categories, the reaction to globalization seems to have varied.

Procter and Gamble (P&G), the most prestigious packaged goods marketer, has reportedly taken the position that "the world brand trend may be going too far. . . . Rather than work toward 'globally standardized' products worldwide, P&G is in the midst of a 'global planning' strategy designed to get products into world markets on a faster timetable."[15] On the other hand, Colgate-Palmolive and Gillette appear to be moving toward a fully global approach.[16]

The same mixed reaction has occurred in the advertising agency business. Saatchi and Saatchi, now the leading world agency, has strongly embraced the "global" concept.[17] McCann Erickson, one of the world's most global agencies in terms of office network, takes a much more cautious approach, warning marketers to ask themselves some serious questions about their products and businesses before "laying down your hard-earned marketing dollars to go global."[18] As Robert James, the president of McCann explained: "While the agency's global philosophy is in agreement with Professor Levitt's theory, . . . McCann doesn't read the situation as global or perish."[19] J. Walter Thompson, one of the oldest international agencies, has as its global mandate—"keep it local."[20] Ted Bates Worldwide advocates: "Think global, act locally." BBDO takes the stance that in spite of the focus on globalization, marketing will continue to operate at four different levels: local, international, multinational, and global." The CEO of Ogilvy and Mather points out that ". . . clearly the global strategy is not meant for every brand."[21]

In the academic world, Professor Philip Kotler of Northwestern has been the most vocal dissenter. He argues, "Levitt thinks a marketer should focus on the similarities nation to nation. I think a marketer should focus on the differences. We've learned that we can sell products if we pay attention to the taste, culture, and buying patterns of the marketplace." It has been reported that other academic colleagues feel Levitt has gone too far in his embrace of global marketing. "It is very rare that among the marketing mix at least one or more variables would not have to be adjusted," says Louis W. Stern, executive director of the Marketing Science Institute. "Levitt loves to exaggerate to make a point." Louis P. Bucklin of the University of California adds, "To think people are similar in terms of social or linguistic concepts is just plain wrong." Dartmouth's Frederick E. Webster questions whether or not even Levitt himself "believes the extreme position he takes."[22]

And so the globalization of markets controversy continues. Where the leading U.S. companies really stand on globalization, no one quite knows. Clearly it is a marketing concept that will continue to be discussed, rehashed, and digested again and again. Whether globalization as defined by Levitt is valid or not, perhaps the most important accomplishment of all has been the focus it has given to the international aspects of U.S. business—an area where

U.S. companies must do better if the U.S. is to survive as an important factor worldwide.

## Is Levitt's Concept New?

Obviously, the idea of the "world brand" did not suddenly start the day Levitt wrote his article. As William Phillips, the head of Ogilvy and Mather, points out, "marketers have traveled an international route for decades and are evolving their efforts to take advantage of new technologies and possible cost savings . . . the idea that all of a sudden Levitt writes a book and discovers global marketing is a superficial revelation of something going on for some time."[23]

Let us now look at the evolution of Levitt's concept.

# 3

# The Evolution of the
# Globalization Concept

Looking back over the last 25 years, it becomes evident that Theodore Levitt
has not turned over completely new ground with his globalization of markets
theory. Rather, Levitt has been successful in putting *timely focus* on several
critical issues that have been discussed over and over in the international marketing literature. During the last 25 years those important recurring issues have
been: convergence of world cultures; universal marketing versus local adaptation; centralized control of marketing versus decentralized control; the need for
improved and more abundant international marketing research.

Some of the key writings which led up to Levitt's current concept are
highlighted in the sections that follow.

## Pre-1960

Since the early 1940s, increasing emphasis has been placed on cross-cultural
research. An excellent example of this was George P. Murdock's search for
cultural universals published in 1945—"The Common Denominators of Culture."[1] In this study, Murdock established a whole list of cultural universals
which he believed were characteristic of any culture even though local expres-
sion and execution might vary:

| | |
|---|---|
| age grading | divination |
| athletic sports | division of labor |
| bodily adornment | dream analysis |
| calendar | education |
| cleanliness training | ethics |
| community organization | etiquette |
| cooking | family feasting |
| cooperative labor | firemaking |
| cosmology | folklore |
| courtship | food taboos |
| dancing | inheritance |
| decorative art | joking |

| | |
|---|---|
| kin groups | property rights |
| language | propitiation of supernatural |
| law | puberty customs |
| marriage | religious rituals |
| mealtime | residence rules |
| medicine | sexual rules |
| modesty about natural functions | soul concepts |
| mourning music | status difference |
| nomenclature | superstition |
| obstetrics | surgery |
| penal sanctions | toolmaking |
| personal names | trade |
| population policy | visiting |
| postnatal care | weaning |
| pregnancy usage | weather control |

From a marketing viewpoint, this work was particularly important because it led off a series of cross-cultural studies, some of which eventually recognized that with increasing communication, travel, and technical developments some national attitudes were gradually becoming more universal.

**The 1960–65 Period**

In 1962 Everett M. Rogers introduced his diffusion of innovations concept— since then widely accepted as classic marketing theory. From an international marketing viewpoint, Rogers' ideas were key because they highlighted the diffusion differences that could exist in different countries at different stages of development. What might be an innovation in one culture could be old hat in another. There could also be great differences in the percentage of the population who might be innovators or early adapters depending on the country's stage of development. Inherent in Rogers' theory, too, was the idea that with countries at the same stage of development, the rate of diffusion for an innovation might be similar.[2]

It was also in 1962 that Ernest Dichter took a provocative stand on universality in his article "The World Customer." Dichter pointed out that a better understanding of cultural anthropology would be an increasingly important tool for competing on a worldwide basis. As he put it, "the basic differences, as well as basic similarities, among consumers in different parts of the world will be essential. They mean that the successful marketer of the future will have to think not of a United States customer nor even a Western European or Atlantic community customer, but of a *world customer*."

Dichter attributed the growth of universality in part to the growth of a large middle class. He outlined six different clusters of countries representing similar stages of development in the growth of a strong middle class. These ranged from the nearly 100 percent middle class Scandinavian countries all the way to the primitive African countries where no middle class existed.

Thus, Ernest Dichter predicted the globalization of markets concept 21 years before Theodore Levitt. As he concluded:

> In most countries I have visited I find that human desires are pretty much alike. . . . Step by step, year by year, we free ourselves more and more from inhibitions, fears and narrow-minded routine thinking. . . . Jets reduce physical distances, international trade and mass communications break down barriers. The world is coming up. The common market will broaden into an Atlantic market and finally into a World Market. In order to participate effectively in this progressive development of mankind, it is essential to have a creative awareness of human desire and its strategy throughout the world—to understand and prepare to serve the new World Customer.[3]

Following Dichter's article, there were several *Journal of Marketing* papers expanding on the idea—particularly in reference to the universality of Europe. Typical of these were Ilmar Roostal's article on "Standardization of Advertising for Western Europe"[4] and Erik Elinder's discussion, "How International Can European Advertising Be?"[5] Both of these articles indicated that increasing universality was possible—at least in Europe.

It was in 1964 that A. H. Maslow established his hierarchy of needs theory. Again from an international marketing viewpoint, this called attention to the differences that could exist among different countries due to their degree of development. The more primitive a culture, the more likely it will be that large segments of the population would be at the lower end of the need hierarchy—physiological and safety. The more developed a culture, the more likely it will be that large population segments would be motivated by self-actualization, esteem, and social motivators. Also inherent in Maslow's theory is a conclusion that among countries at the same stage of development, the need motivators for large segments of the population might be similar.[6]

In 1965 Millard Pryor addressed the issue of control in international planning—decentralization versus centralization. In his article "Planning a Worldwide Business," he highlighted the current dominance of local control. As he expressed it, "Marketing is conspicuous by its absence from the functions which can be planned at the corporate headquarters level. It is in this phase of overseas business activity that the variations in social patterns and the subtlety of local conditions have the most pronounced effect on basic business strategy and tactics." Most importantly, Pryor went on to stress that in the future, an interactive approach combining global and local considerations would be far superior to either centralized or decentralized control.[7]

## The 1966–71 Period

In 1966 James E. Lee established the concept of SRC—self reference criteria. This was defined as an unconscious reference to one's own cultural values in making decisions. In his article "Cultural Analysis in Overseas Operations," Lee set up four steps which would help eliminate SRC. The net impact of Lee's concept, therefore, put new emphasis on taking into account cultural differences in making marketing decisions.[8]

In 1967 Howard Perlmutter defined the basic marketing philosophies that companies had in dealing with overseas business. He described an *ethnocentric* approach as a belief that the home country approach is best. Perlmutter pointed out that since the early days, many U.S. companies involved in export had taken this approach.

Perlmutter defined a *polycentric* approach as the belief that host countries are key—that it is necessary to adapt totally to local cultures and practices. He pointed out that many European companies have tended to follow this approach and hence have ended up with a "series of host country oriented units."

Perlmutter's final definition, *geocentric,* described an integrated world strategy which advocates that similarities and differences across the world can be understood and dealt with on their merits. So Perlmutter, 16 years before Levitt's article, was defining a global strategy that tried to maximize consumer value and minimize company costs by using an interactive worldwide approach.[9]

It was also in 1967 that Arthur C. Fatt took a bold and controversial stand in his *Journal of Marketing* article, "The Danger of Local International Advertising." Fatt was openly impatient in his criticism of those marketers who overemphasized local adaptation. His major contention was that "even in the U.S., despite our language, we have a heterogeneous market. . . . [N]o product or service is sold to everyone in any country, . . . no single country is a single unified market but is composed of market segments, each with its own characteristics." Fatt felt, therefore, that the real issue was to seek out common market segments regardless of national boundaries. He challenged whether a company gained a larger market share "by automatically changing every theme to suit so called individual characteristics of every country."

Fatt concluded that "political boundaries do not circumscribe psychological or emotional attitudes. . . . [A]s the marketing concept spreads around the world, it will lead to more effective planning, probing and testing, and thus universal advertising appeals will be regarded with greater objectivity." Again, 5 years after Dichter and 16 years before Levitt, here was another advocate of globalization.[10]

The year following Fatt's article, Robert Bartels echoed Fatt in advancing the concept of *total* world marketing. In his *Journal of Marketing* article "Are Domestic and International Marketing Dissimilar?" Bartels stressed that "emphasis on the inherent similarities rather than the differences will enable a better understanding of the nature of a foreign market by U.S. firms. To the extent that these similarities are perceived, they will make possible the formulation of more integrated marketing theory, business structure, and academic offerings." In his conclusions, Bartels made a strong plea for globalization by advocating that "in marketing products around the world, we must think universally."

While Bartels agreed that we cannot ignore differences in cultures, his main point was that "as space and time shrink even more and as more and more products come into the market, basic universal appeals will be more effective."[11]

In 1969 Donnelly and Ryans surveyed 175 nondurable goods companies to see if Fatt's call for universal advertising was being followed. Their article, "Global Advertising: A Call as Yet Unanswered," for the *Journal of Marketing,* reported that most advertisers felt their international advertising should be adapted for each local country. The study showed, therefore, that Fatt's globalization concept was ahead of its time as far as practical company application was concerned.[12]

That same year John Ryans, Jr., echoed this same conclusion in his article "Is It Too Soon to Put a Tiger in Every Tank?" In discussing Fatt's concept of universal advertising, Ryans concluded that "few, if any, would disagree with the view that advances in communications, education, etc., will ultimately create an atmosphere where the common advertising approach will be the rule rather than the exception. However, adoption of such an approach today is premature and advertisers should make use of it with caution."[13]

In 1969 Warren Keegan supported the concept that products and communications sometimes had to be altered overseas, and he defined the strategic alternatives for changing the product-communications mix when introducing a product into a new country. In a *Journal of Marketing* article Keegan established five basic strategies. An introduction with no change was defined as a straight product-communication extension. Products involving some adaptation were defined as either a product extension with a communication adaptation or as a product adaptation with a communication extension. A complete change in the mix was defined as a dual adaptation strategy. Keegan's fifth strategy called for a completely new product invention along with new communication.[14]

Also in 1969, John Fayerweather published *International Business Management: A Conceptual Framework,* which set up a framework for dealing with the unifying and differentiating influences in each country. His contention was that in each situation there were similar aspects which tended to unify the strategy on a given product. At the same time there were unique aspects calling for differentiation and adaptation. Fayerweather advocated a balance in analyzing the marketing program. He believed it was critical for the global manager to know the similarities and the differences and to sense what should not be changed and what should be.[15]

In 1970 R. J. Aylmer did research among European affiliates of nine U.S.-based multinational companies to study how much local management autonomy was granted on critical marketing mix decisions. Although there was considerable discussion at this time about an integrated, global approach, this study showed that as a practical matter local adaptation and dominance in decision making was frequent. Primary authority rested with local management in

86 percent of the 84 advertising programs observed; in 74 percent of the 84 pricing decisions studied; and 61 percent of the 86 distribution decisions covered. Only in basic product design did headquarters management tend to dominate.[16]

In 1971 Warren Keegan continued to emphasize the importance of an "interactive marketing program designed to respond not only to market differences but to similarities as well" as a key "source of major international operating efficiencies." His article in the *Columbia Journal of World Business* made a strong case for the fact that "an interactive marketing program, designed to respond to similarities and differences . . . can be the source of major international operating synergies. In this context, synergy occurs when the effectiveness of an integrated unit is greater than the sum of the capabilities of the individual operating units."[17]

It was also in 1971 that S. Prakash Sethi advanced the idea of cluster analysis in his classic *Journal of Marketing Research* article "Comparative Cluster Analysis for World Markets."[18] Using key criteria such as income per capita, market size, and stage of market development, Sethi clustered foreign markets' environments into homogeneous groups. These groups resulted in clear within-group similarities *and* between-group differences. This cluster analysis concept has become increasingly important as a part of the globalization of markets idea.

**The 1972–77 Period**

In 1972 Warren Keegan made extensive use of the cluster analysis concept in his classic article "A Conceptual Framework for Multinational Marketing." Keegan stressed that there are three basic dimensions of multinational marketing which differentiate it from domestic marketing. The first dimension, Keegan said, was *environmental,* which called for a sensitivity to differences and similarities in each foreign environment. The second dimension he called *crossing boundaries,* which involved the different terms of sale for each country—tariffs, legal restrictions, quotas, etc. And the third dimension Keegan defined as *simultaneous marketing in more than one country,* which created great leverage for marketing programs, systems transfers, and people transfers. Keegan then laid out a conceptual framework for dealing with the international marketing problem on an integrated basis—covering environmental analysis, strategic planning, structure, operational planning and control.[19]

Once again in 1974 the concept of grouping world markets for product planning was expanded on by Eugene D. Jaffe. Under the auspices of the American Marketing Association, Jaffe laid out a whole cluster analysis process in his book *Grouping: A Strategy for International Marketing.* This again suggested that there were large clusters of countries that could be dealt with by a more universal marketing program.[20]

In the winter of 1974 Stewart Britt conducted a survey which showed that in spite of the considerable discussion about common marketing programs, most companies wanted their nondomestic programs adapted to each locale. The highlight of Britt's article, "Standardizing Advertising for the International Market," was a systematic information collection method which hopefully would indicate where a specific product could use a standardized approach. This utilized a whole series of questions based on consumption patterns (purchase and usage), psychosocial characteristics (attitudes toward brand, product, or service), and cultural criteria (restrictions, stigmas, and traditions of society that affect product usage).[21]

In 1975 Robert Green, William Cunningham, and Isabella Cunningham made a study of standardized advertising in the consumer goods category. As reported in their article, "The Effectiveness of Standardized Global Advertising," college students were surveyed in the U.S., France, Brazil, and India. The study concluded that there existed a wide difference in appeals among students in the different countries and that standardized advertising, therefore, would be far less effective than advertising adapted for the local scene.[22]

On the other hand, that same year a study made by Ralph Sorenson and Ulrich Wiechmann indicated there was a trend toward a high degree of marketing standardization among European subsidiaries of selected multinational companies. Their article, "How Multinationals View Marketing Standardization," showed that the highest degree of standardization was in the areas of product characteristics, brand names, packaging, and basic advertising message. A lower degree of standardization was present in the areas of pricing, media allocation, sales promotion, and advertising execution.

The thrust of the article's conclusion was well expressed by this statement from one of the headquarter's executives interviewed. While the executive felt "total standardization of all the elements of the marketing mix was hardly thinkable," he did believe that the process of approaching, analyzing, and solving a marketing problem could be standardized on an international basis. As he put it, "If decision making is done in each country according to the same intellectual process, it can be more easily understood by headquarters management; a standard process eliminating guesses on the subjective side of marketing permits one to arrive more easily at the standardization of certain elements of the marketing mix."[23]

In 1975 David R. McIntyre made a strong case for a universal product positioning in his article "Multinational Positioning Strategy." Using several consumer products as examples, McIntyre predicted the increased use of worldwide strategies. As he concluded, "The world is growing smaller all the time. Television satellite broadcasting, inexpensive group travel plans, etc., have all contributed to this shrink phenomenon. In the process, we have found that there is really very little difference between worldwide consumers. They all want quality products which will enhance their personal prestige at an affordable price. This is the universality of the average consumer with disposable income. Advertising strategy which has proven to be successful in one country has a fairly good chance of being successful in another. That's what multinational positioning is all about."[24]

In 1975 Robert Green and Eric Langeard did a study reported in the *Journal of Marketing* comparing cross-national consumer habits and innovator characteristics in France and in the U.S. Their conclusion was that important differences did exist and that more effective international research was needed. They pointed out that even though France and the U.S. were similar in many ways economically there were definite differences which "could be attributed to social and environmental factors." Green and Langeard pointed out that the study "emphasized the need for further theoretical and empirical cross-national research to achieve a better understanding of the relationships between buyer behavior and environmental forces. . . . International marketing at the level of sophistication currently practiced domestically in the United States will only be possible when more is known about the behavior of consumers out of this country."[25]

In 1976 Edward T. Hall wrote *Beyond Culture*—a current update on changing cultural patterns.[26] Hall emphasized that culture was not innate but rather a learned set of beliefs and behavioral codes.

He also stressed that the various facets of culture were interrelated. "Touch a culture in one area and all areas are affected." Therefore, the installation of television programing into a culture would have a profound effect on all other components of the culture.

Hall went on to point out that the growing profusion of automobiles, convenience foods, disposable packages, and other articles in Europe and Japan suggests "that many or perhaps even most consumer products have universal appeal." Hall advanced the idea that "these products will be purchased in any country regardless of cultural differences when disposable income reaches a high enough level."

It was in his book, too, that Hall introduced the concept of high and low context cultures. In *high context* cultures (Japan, Arab states), the context of the situation is highly important: who you are; associations; background; basic values of those communicating. More meaning is attached to the situation than the actual words spoken or written. In a *low context* culture (U.S., East Germany), words are more explicit, more abundant, and more critical. The context of the situation is far less important. In low context cultures, written contracts and legal verbage are extremely critical.

In 1977 Warren Keegan's article, "Strategic Marketing: International Diversification Versus National Concentration," predicted further growth of the multinational company with a world viewpoint. Keegan quoted several authorities who foresaw an end to national boundaries. He pointed out that George Ball, for example, believed the multinational corporation was a "modern concept designed to meet the requirements of a modern age; the nation state was a very old-fashioned idea and badly adapted to serve the needs of our present complex world."

Sidney Rolfe was quoted as saying that "the phenomenal progress in communications and transportation technologies has created an interdependence of human activity that has rendered national boundaries obsolete." Arnold Toynbee, expressing a similar view, sees "the multinational corporation as an institution that fills a vacuum in an increasingly interdependent world economy."

As Keegan so aptly put it, "Those who see an expanding future for the multinational company are assuming the continuation of the technological, social, and political shrinkage of the globe which has been underway for centuries and which has been accelerated dramatically during the past three decades. This shrinkage is creating in an increasing number of industries, . . . a handful of giant worldwide companies which find it increasingly feasible to manage activities in every corner of the globe."

Keegan clustered international markets into five groups or scenarios based on host country stage of development. He also advanced the idea that "a serious limitation to multinational company growth was host country nationalism and the perception of unfair distribution of gains between home and host countries."

Keegan's conclusion was that "the multinational companies most broadly define their own corporate interests to include current aspirations of both home and host governments and societies." Keegan's opinion was that if multinational companies did this, "further expansion of this important world institution can be expected."[27]

That same year, Yoram Wind and Howard Perlmutter wrote a paper emphasizing the great need for improved multinational research. This discussion "On the Identification of Frontier Issues in Multinational Marketing" stressed, for example, the neglect in the consumer research area. As they put it, "the study and understanding of consumer behavior in various countries is an essential input to the development of any multinational marketing strategy and theory. The multinational environment can provide a rich setting for the study of similarities and differences among consumers and their responses to marketing variables."

Another example of much needed multinational research discussed by the authors was the area of multinational marketing concepts and models. They pointed out that marketing concepts such as target marketing, market segmentation, and product positioning were obviously applicable to international marketing. However, even though the approach to solving marketing problems should be the same regardless of geographical boundaries, little research was available to substantiate this. As they put it, "further work is required to determine whether and how to adjust the domestically oriented marketing concepts to the multinational environment." Certainly more research was needed to determine under what conditions *standardized* marketing strategy can be applied.[28]

**The 1978–83 Period**

In 1978 James Killough emphasized the virtues of universal advertising in his *Harvard Business Review* article "Improved Payoffs from Transnational Advertising. The study conducted for the article revealed considerable executive skepticism toward transnational advertising. Most of the executives interviewed felt that a strong selling proposition could be transferred successfully about 50 percent of the time. On the other hand, they felt that the creative presentation of the proposition may not travel well. The executives believed that to have an international campaign, it was essential to have a brand or product with a truly global market.[29]

That same year, Dean Peebles, John Ryans, Jr., and Ivan Vernon addressed the problem of coordinating international advertising in their article for the *Journal of Marketing*. To avoid the "standardized versus localized" debate, the authors recommended an integrated, programed approach that takes into account the similarities and the differences but with a global emphasis.

After describing in detail the managed approach used internationally by Goodyear, the authors came to the conclusion that the

> communication process and the other safeguards built into the programed management approach, such as the creative workshop and the required independent market research, help to assure that effective campaigns are developed and that valid corporate policies and objectives are implemented. The programed management approach represents a hybrid prototype, a cross between close corporate control and local option management. The result is a product of teamwork, a blending of effort by corporate, local market, and agency representatives. The end result is an effective international advertising campaign—one well designed to meet local market conditions, and, yet, one that is in harmony with long-range corporate objectives.[30]

In 1978 and 1979, Igal Ayal and Jehiel Zif wrote articles for the *Columbia Journal of World Business*[31] and the *Journal of Marketing*,[32] on expansion strategies in multinational marketing. One important strategy recognized by the authors was the global approach which called for a concentration on one or two product segments as a world brand in a widely diversified number of countries. Ayal and Zif point out that this strategy works best, of course, when there is a low need for product and communication adaptation.

In 1979 Paul Michell made a strong case for adjustments in local marketing programs due to variations in what he termed the "infrastructure" in each country. His article, "Infrastructures and International Marketing," laid out six areas that necessitate responsiveness to the local scene: economy, technology, distribution, mass communications, national culture, and government.[33]

That same year, an article in the *Harvard Business Review*, "Problems that Plague Multinational Marketers," emphasized the difficulty of coordinating and staffing an effective international marketing program. The authors, Ulrich

Wiechmann and Lewis G. Pringle, pointed out that "what really bothers marketing executives in the home office is the failure of marketing managers in the foreign subsidiaries to develop long-term strategy. And what bothers the subsidiary managers is overemphasis by the parent company on short-term financial performance. In other words, one organizational level is the principal problem of the other."

The study showed that at the headquarters level concerns fall into three categories:(1) shortage of qualified persons to staff the international operations; (2) subsidiary managers' deficiencies in planning and marketing know-how; and (3) shortcomings in the communications and control processes of the multinational enterprise.

At the subsidiary level, the study showed that the main concerns were: (1) too many constraints imposed by headquarters; (2) too little attention given by headquarters to local differences; and (3) inadequate information from headquarters.[34]

And so it seemed that after 25 years of discussion, many of the same problems of local control versus headquarters control still existed in the international marketing community.

In 1980 Michael Colvin, Roger Heeler, and Jim Thorpe advanced the case for a more standardized marketing approach. As they expressed it in their *Journal of Marketing* article, "In practical terms the task of developing a marketing strategy per country is daunting, even for companies with large resources. Numerous research programs are required in different countries at different times and these must be repeated each time a new strategy option is to be tested." The authors go on to point out that "the current trend is toward 'pattern standardization'; whereby a strategy is designed from the outset to be susceptible to extensive modification to suit local conditions, while maintaining sufficient common elements to minimize the drain on resources and management time."[35]

Later that year, Michael E. Porter in his book *Cases in Competitive Strategy* emphasized overall cost leadership as a growing strategy for marketers.[36] Three years later, Levitt's globalization concept placed great emphasis on the cost leadership which can be gained with an integrated global approach. The cost savings derived from the economy of scale in global marketing is one of the key leverage points advocated by Levitt.

Starting in the 1980s, there was much more consistent emphasis on an integrated approach to international marketing and how to solve the complex problems involved. In 1981 Harry Davis, Susan Douglas, and Calvin Silk tackled the problem of improved international research. Their *Journal of Marketing* article pointed out that "a potential threat to conclusions drawn from cross-national marketing surveys is that arising from differences in measure reliability. In a five-country study, between-sample reliability differentials were uncovered that appeared to be related to the type of measurement used but not to particular national samples or language groups."

The authors stressed that "a key issue that invariably arises in connection with these multinational research efforts is whether observed similarities or differences between markets are, in fact, real." The article points out that "few experienced in primary data collection would question the proposition that the possible threats to validity increase dramatically as the number and diversity of countries encompassed by a consumer research project is expanded." The authors then further discuss the specific technical research problems involved.[37]

The following year a group lead by Jehiel Zif and Hiram Barksdale did a six-country cross-national study on consumer attitudes toward marketing practices, consumerism and government regulation. The assumption of the study reported in the *Columbia Journal of World Business* was that attitudes in each country would be related to the stage of development of the consumer movement. To the surprise of the authors, the results indicated a remarkable universality of attitude across the board whether it was Australia, Israel, Norway, England, Canada, or the U.S. As reported in the study, for example, "the majority of consumers in all six countries acknowledge that the products required by the average family are conveniently available. Also consumers everywhere express concern about the high prices of goods and services despite the wide variations in inflation rates and price levels. Consumers also conceded that many of the mistakes they make in buying are the result of their own carelessness and ignorance. Product quality is another universal concern. . . . Negative attitudes toward advertising are registered by consumers in all six nations. Respondents simply do not accept advertising at face value; nor do they believe that advertised products are superior in quality to unadvertised ones. Finally, there is a strong feeling in all countries that government has a responsibility to safeguard the rights of consumers."[38]

In his book *Multinational Marketing Management* prepared in the early 1980s for the 1984 edition, Warren Keegan was again a forerunner in stressing the value of the interactive, integrated approach to international marketing. He explained that the global approach "is superior to either the standardized or the local plan because it draws on the strengths of each of these approaches in planning to formulate a synthesis. . . . Under the interactive marketing planning approach, subsidiaries are responsible for identifying the unique characteristics of their market. . . . Headquarters . . . is responsible for establishing a broad strategic framework for planning. . . . In addition, headquarters must coordinate and rationalize the product design, advertising, pricing and distribution activities of each subsidiary operation."

Keegan points out that "each decision must stand on its own merit, but there are significant opportunities for the improvement of performance and cost savings by concentrating certain activities at one location. For example, many companies have successfully centralized the preparation of advertising appeals at world or regional headquarters. Another activity that can be done in one location is product design. Information and design criteria need to come from the world, the design itself can be done by one design team in a single location."

Keegan stresses that "the global plan is neither the product of the sub-sidiary nor the product of headquarters. It is neither 'top down' nor 'bottom up' but rather an interactive product that combines input from both the global and local perspective. This balance is essential if the plan is to approximate the ob-jective of global optimization as opposed to national suboptimization. . . ."[39]

In their 1982 article "How Global Companies Win Out," Thomas Hout, Michael E. Porter, and Eileen Rudder reaffirmed the entire premise of the globalization of markets. This *Harvard Business Review* article stresses the di-mension of international competitiveness and the necessity for adopting a more global approach as a means of survival. The authors point out that with the growing vulnerability to increased foreign competition, there are companies that have made great progress in offsetting this threat by adopting a new view-point.

> These companies rely on global strategies to succeed in today's world. That calls for a com-pany to think of the world as one market instead of a collection of national markets and sometimes requires decisions as unconventional as accepting projects with low [return on in-vestments] because of their competitive payoff. An organization with such global focus for-mulates long-term strategy for the company as a whole and then orchestrates the strategies of local subsidiaries accordingly. . . . To succeed an international company may need to change from a multidomestic competitor, which allows individual subsidiaries to compete in-dependently in different markets, to a global organization which puts its entire worldwide system . . . against the competition. The global company . . . tries to control leverage points, from production scale economies to foreign competitors sources of cash flow. . . . By taking unconventional action, such as lowering prices . . . in key markets, the company makes the competitors' response more expensive and difficult.

The authors acknowledge that not all companies can or even should em-bark on a global strategy. Such a strategy requires a number of unconventional approaches to managing international business which may not be appropriate for everyone. Going global is complex, difficult, and requires a whole new way of thinking. For example, it may require major investments with slow payoffs or financial performance targets that vary widely among foreign subsidiaries. It may require product lines deliberately overdesigned or underpriced in some markets. It may necessitate construction of production facilities in both high and low labor cost countries. It requires a view of country-by-country market positions as interdependent elements in a worldwide portfolio.

The conclusion of the paper leads very logically to Theodore Levitt's globalization of markets concept that was presented in the spring of the follow-ing year. As the article puts it, "although adopting a global strategy is risky, many companies can dramatically improve their positions by fundamentally changing the way they plan, control and operate their businesses. . . . If the company can successfully execute a global strategy, it may find itself joining the ranks of the truly successful international companies. Whether they be Japanese, American, European, or otherwise, the strategic threat that ties together companies like IBM, Matsushita, DuPont, and Michelin clearly shows that the rules of the international competitive game have changed."[40]

In May 1983 Levitt published his much discussed globalization concept both as an article in the *Harvard Business Review* and as a chapter in his book, *The Marketing Imagination*.[41] The thrust of this milestone work has already been reviewed in chapter 2.

## The 1984–86 Period

In 1985 Sandra Huszagh, Richard Fox, and Ellen Day tried to pin down the practicality of Levitt's globalization theory. Their study addressed three questions: (1) which foreign markets were similar, (2) which products have a potential for global marketing by having similar acceptance rates, and (3) are there product characteristics which explain these acceptance rates? Twenty-one developed nations were clustered into five groups using cluster analysis of twelve economic factors. Twenty-seven different products were then studied in these countries in terms of penetration and consumer perception. The study indicated "that some products clearly do not lend themselves to a global marketing approach" while "the potential for global marketing does exist for several, specific product categories." Their conclusion suggested that the answer to the global marketing debate was to combine "global vision" with a "local touch."[42]

That same year, Howard Perlmutter, working with Balaji Chakravarthy, updated his theory on management's international philosophy—this time adding regiocentric to his previous definitions of ethnocentric, polycentric, and geocentric. Regiocentric was described as "a predisposition that tries to blend the interests of the parent with that of the subsidiaries at least on a limited, regional basis." The major thrust of the paper was to point out that a multinational's path in strategic planning depended on (1) the "economic imperative" which determines where to locate the different elements of the value chain for the business; (2) the "political imperative" which depends on host company demands; and (3) the company's own "strategic predisposition."[43]

In 1985 Gary Hamel and C. K. Prahalad asked in their *Harvard Business Review* article "Do You Really Have a Global Strategy?" They pleaded that "executives must look beyond lower costs and product standardization to think in new ways about world competition." The authors stressed that the global operation offers leverage which allows that company to fight competition on all world fronts. As they put it, "Global competitors are not battling simply for world volume but also for the cash flow to support new product development, investment in core technologies, and world distribution. Companies that nestle safely in their home beds will be at an increasing resource (if not a cost) disadvantage. They will be unable to marshal the forces required for a defense of the home market." The paper concluded that "to build organizations capable of conceiving and executing complex global strategies, top managers must develop the new analytic approaches and organizational arrangements on which our competitive future rests."[44]

Another important paper that year was published by Philip Kotler and Somkid Jatusripitak. "Strategic Global Marketing: Lessons from the Japanese" shows how the Japanese had used global marketing techniques to gain dominance in many product categories. As the authors pointed out, "Japanese firms today are no longer merely exporting firms but are multinational firms playing for high stakes in the global game of international business. . . . [G]lobal marketing has greatly benefited Japan and is key to its trade success." The paper reviews the specific strategy used by the Japanese to expand globally—a strategy that included entry into developing countries to gain economy of scale and entry into trial developed markets to gain experience. The authors show how the Japanese also benefit greatly by having (1) a worldwide decentralized production system and (2) profit leverage which allows them to finance marketing efforts in specific areas from world profits.[45]

In 1986 John Quelch and Edward Hoff probed the area of implementation of a global strategy. "Customizing Global Marketing" tries to lay out a framework for companies to help them structure the different areas of the marketing function for a global operation. As they put it, "The big issue today is not whether to go global but how to tailor the global marketing concept to fit each business."[46]

In the same year Roberto Friedmann proposed a simple psychological testing system to measure the meaning of products in different cultures as a way of simplifying the decision whether to standardize or adapt. His paper in the *Columbia Journal of World Business* outlined a measurement using one-word associations elicited within a 70-second time limit. Responses were then clustered to give a psychological profile of the product meaning. Friedmann proposes that "the psychological meaning of products . . . gives a measurable construct that can help in determining the degree of standardization, if any, that international marketers incorporate into their strategies."[47]

A new book later in 1986, *Competition in Global Industries,* edited by Michael Porter, was designed to help guide companies amid increasing global competitiveness. The book stresses that each company and product category can be very different in its dealing with international marketing strategy. As Porter puts it, "The distinctive issues in international strategy have to do with the location where each activity in the product value chain is performed—and the coordination of these activities in different countries. . . . At one extreme is the country-centered strategy in which a company employs a highly dispersed configuration of activities in different countries . . . making little or no effort at coordination. In contrast, the simplest global strategy would be to concentrate as many activities as possible in one country. . . . But since the company must consider each activity of the value chain separately, there are a multitude of possible global strategies."

Porter points out that there are four broad types of strategy—global cost leadership, global product differentiation, global segmentation serving only one world segment, and protected markets where local investments are shielded by government impediments to global competition. The book clearly stresses the complexity of a global strategy and the great demands its places on managers.[48]

## The Future of the Globalization Concept

Certainly this review of the past has revealed that Levitt, in advancing his globalization of markets concept, was not breaking completely new ground. Rather, he was putting new, dramatic insight and focus on what many experts had been discussing for years. Aside from the strong and concise statement of his premise, there were two other very important factors that helped bring wide attention to Levitt's work. First, his writing came at a time when U.S. multinationals faced the severest competition they had ever experienced from foreign competitors. The subject of U.S. competitiveness was foremost in people's minds. Second, it came at a time when the much debated cultural convergence was, in fact, more and more of a reality—certainly at least among large segments of the industrialized world. Twenty years before, Ernest Dichter had been ahead of his time. Theodore Levitt was much closer to the mark.

As is often the case, the *timeliness* of Levitt's writing has been a critical factor in its success. The important question now is just where does the globalization take us for the future? Whether or not one accepts the standardization of marketing mix elements, the true test of globalization is how effective it will be for new product expansion. If, in fact, the concept of "world brands" can be harnessed successfully for new product development, then Levitt's globalization concept will be maximized in its value to companies as an effective marketing strategy.

# 4

# Global New Product Development

In a heated discussion between Theodore Levitt and several marketing executives, there was one clear area of agreement. They all agreed that the development of products specifically designed for global markets made more sense than forcing old products into some kind of universal mold. The report on the discussion stated: "The roundtable thought it was wiser to create a new product for global consumption rather than to take on an existing brand with its established characteristics and try to sell it the same way everywhere.[1]

It is my belief that the future success of U.S. companies will depend very much on their ability to launch new products for the world market. Therefore, the truest test of Levitt's globalization concept will be how well the strategy applies to new product development. Even for those companies now globalizing existing brands, the real issue will be how well globalization works to make their new product effort successful worldwide.

As I have previously stated, it is my premise that most U.S. multinational companies today are ignoring the concept of global new product development. This rejection in one of the most vital areas of company performance is surprising. It is even more baffling considering that a greater number of companies are starting to utilize the globalization strategy on established brands.

## The Evolution of Current New Product Development Practices

During the 1970s new product development was seen by most U.S. companies as the key answer to future domestic growth. In this period, many companies staffed large new product departments; trade groups such as the American Marketing Association and the Association of National Advertisers promoted frequent seminars/workshops; new product development literature proliferated. The 1970s, with its concept of positioning and its almost fanatical concern with shorter life cycles and rapid change, was truly an action era for new product work.

Before the 1970s there were few books devoted to new product development. In terms of theory, new product development was usually dealt with in

Table 2.   The Most Significant Texts on New Product Development,
1970s and 1980s

1970   Peter Kraushar. *New Products and Diversification*. Brandon/Systems Press.
1972   Delmar W. Karger and Robert G. Murdick. *New Product Venture Management*. Gordon and Breach.
1972   Donald H. Slocum. *New Venture Methodology*. American Management Association.
1973   Stephen King. *Developing New Brands*. John Wiley and Sons.
1974   Robert R. Rothberg. *Corporate Strategy and Product Innovation*. Free Press.
1974   Eberhard E. Scheuing. *New Product Management*. Dryden Press.
1974   William H. Shames. *Venture Management*. Free Press.
1977   David Midgley. *Innovation and New Product Marketing*. John Wiley and Sons.
1977   Robert R. Rothberg and Douglas W. Mellott, Jr. *New Product Planning*. American Marketing Association.
1977   E. Spitz. *New Product Planning*. Petrolli Center.
1978   Robert D. Hisrich and Michael P. Peters. *Marketing a New Product: Its Planning, Development and Control*. Benjamin/Cummings.
1980   *Management of the New Product Function*. Association of National Advertisers.
1980   Glen L. Urban and J. Hauser. *Design and Marketing of New Products*. Prentice-Hall.
1981   Frederick Buggie. *New Product Development Strategies*. AMACOM.
1982   Milton D. Rosenau, Jr. *Innovation: Managing the Development of Profitable New Products*. Lifetime Learning Publications.
1984   Robert D. Hisrich and Michael P. Peters. *Marketing Decisions for New and Mature Products*. Charles E. Merrill.
1985   George Gruenwald. *New Product Development*. Crain Books.
1987   C. Merle Crawford. *New Products Management*. Richard D. Irwin.
1987   Glen L. Urban, John R. Hauser, and Nikhilesh Dholakia. *Essentials of New Product Management*. Prentice-Hall.

a small section of standard marketing texts. But starting in the 1970s and on into the 1980s, a number of recognized books on the subject emerged. The most significant of these books are shown in table 2.

These texts as well as other new product literature reveal that during the 1970s and on into the 1980s the procedures and methods recommended for effective new product development programs became much more defined and standardized.

Table 3 shows a comparison of Stephen King's new product development model from the 1970s versus the Booz, Allen and Hamilton model for the 1980s. The comparison highlights two important characteristics about the new product development area as practiced by U.S. consumer goods companies. First, very little basic change in philosophy, methodology, or organization has emerged in the 1980s. The only modification in the '80s has perhaps been the greater emphasis on up-front strategic planning and the refinement of research techniques. Second, very little, if any, attention has been given to international new product development per se. The basic assumption seems to be that new product development is limited to national boundaries and, as such, deals with the home country engaged in the program.

Table 5. Comparison of New Product Development Models—
1970s vs. 1980s

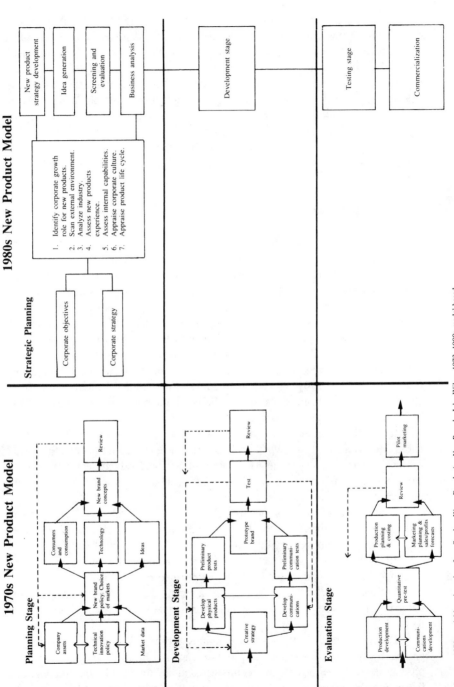

**1970s New Product Model**

**1980s New Product Model**

Sources: 1970s model based on chart from Stephen King, *Developing New Brands*, John Wiley, 1973; 1980s model based

Perhaps the newest thinking in new product development has been the concept of a nonsequential approach instead of the step by step methodology advanced by Stephen King or Booz, Allen in table 3. Hirotaka Takeuchi and Ikujiro Nonaka, in their article "The New Product Development Game," point out that "some companies are realizing that the old, sequential approach to developing new products simply won't get the job done. Instead, companies in Japan and the United States are using a holistic method . . . forming a fast and flexible method for new product development."[2] While this thinking calls for a refreshing and innovative change, it deals with new product development as though it were a domestic problem and assumes the function is bounded by national boundaries.

**Emphasis on National Boundaries**

The lack of emphasis on global or even international new product development is evident in the latest studies from the field. For example, about a year after Levitt's landmark article appeared, the Association of National Advertisers did an extensive study among its members on new product development.[3] The conclusions of this research showed that the majority of companies were pursuing the same approach advanced by the Booz, Allen model. Even with the great attention being focused at the time on globalization, the study did not deal with global new product development. Nor does it cover international new product procedures of any type. Again the assumption seems to be that new product development is limited by national boundaries. International rollouts come only after the brand has been successful in the home country—usually the U.S. for U.S. consumer goods companies.

It is interesting, for example, to look at the area of new product conferences and seminars to see whether or not global new product development was a current topic. Typical is the Association of National Advertisers new product workshop held in New York in 1986 (fig. 1). Global, or even international new product development was not covered.

Perhaps one of the most prestigious new product development programs is that sponsored by the American Management Association (fig. 2). Here again, the material does not cover global new product development. Even the suggestions for who should attend clearly does not include international marketing personnel. A new product conference was planned by the American Marketing Association for early 1987. Again, the agenda, the prestigious speakers involved, and the emphasis of the conference were domestically oriented in focus.

The programs of all these associations are excellent and are highly regarded by business leaders. The programs are advanced as the latest in new product development issues and techniques and are attended by executives from the country's leading marketing companies. Yet, these programs are only re-

Figure 1.   American Association of National Advertisers New Product Marketing Workshop

**Program for the**
# A.N.A.
# New Product
# Marketing Workshop

**Innovation vs. Imitation: How to Win Big**
**By Coming in First...Or Second...**
**Or Third**

A one-day update for marketing executives
on practices that are being used to increase the
effectiveness and payout of new product programs.

**September 10, 1986**

The Plaza Hotel
New York City

---

**8:00 a.m.**
Registration and coffee, Ballroom Foyer

**8.45 a.m.**
**Welcome and Opening Remarks,** Grand Ballroom
Presiding:

**Peter Van Brunt,** Director
of Marketing
Towel & Tissue Division,
James River Corporation
Chair, A.N.A. New Product
Marketing Committee

**Robert H. FitzSimmons,**
Vice President,
Product Management
Dorsey Laboratories,
Division of Sandoz, Inc.
Program Chair

**9:00 a.m.**
**Winning By Getting There First—A Corporate
Strategy**
**Daniel L. Santangelo,** Vice President, Group
General Manager
Soup and Dry Foods Business Units
Campbell Soup Company

Dan represents a corporate philosophy that holds that leading
the field with an innovative new product is the road to success.
He joined Campbell in 1977 as Manager of Marketing Research
for the Swanson Frozen Foods Division. He then moved rapidly
up the corporate marketing ranks through planning, marketing
and general management positions to his present post, to which
he was promoted last year.

**How To Win At The Bank When You're Not
Number One**
**Peter J. Flatow,** President and Chief Operating Officer
BrainReserve, Inc.

Peter holds that you can follow up on a successful new product
launch from another company and improve on it, and gives
examples to prove the thesis. He joined BrainReserve in 1986
after a distinguished career in new product and business
development. He was Director of Corporate Development for
Bristol-Myers; Vice President, New Product Development for
B-M's Drackett Company; Marketing Manager for Lever
Brothers' bar soaps and laundry detergents, and had served
with American Can, H.J. Heinz and Johnson & Johnson.

**Creative Strategies For New Products**
**Hall "Cap" Adams, Jr.,** Chairman and Chief
Executive Officer
Leo Burnett U.S.A.

The creative strategies that work for the first product into the
market may not be good for the second or third brand in. Cap
Adams draws on his experience with such Burnett clients as
Philip Morris and Keebler to illustrate the differences. With
Burnett since 1960, Cap has been involved in account
management and strategy development with several of the
agency's major clients.

**What's Innovative in Your Product Category?**
**Donald Carpenter,** President
Product Initiatives U.S.

Speaking from the experiences of a firm that counsels major
companies in the identification, development and assessment of
new product opportunities, Don will describe the insights
derived from The Innovation Index, which identifies emerging
trends in new products. Among his points is the fact that
innovation jumps from one category to another, often with even
more success than the original.

**Unlocking The Corporate Mind for Creativity**
**John M. Keil,** Executive Vice President
Director of Creative Development
DFS/Dorland Worldwide

Creativity has been a career for Jack. From his beginning as a
radio scriptwriter and actor, he has never been far from

the advertising creative scene. His book, "The Creative
Mystique, How to Manage It, Nurture It and Make It Pay,"
published last year by John Wiley & Sons, answers the question
"Is it possible for creativity and management to co-exist in a
mutually profitable environment?" with a definite "Yes." He will
present his hard-won knowledge of how this is accomplished.

**11:30 p.m.**
**A Panel Discussion With Morning Speakers**
Moderated by the noted marketing columnist of the
*Chicago Tribune:* **George Lazarus**

**12:30 p.m.**
Reception and Luncheon, Terrace Room
**Featured Luncheon Speaker:**
**Bob Costas,** NBC Sports Commentator

Recently honored as National Sportscaster of the Year for
1985, Bob has demonstrated his informative and entertaining
style as both a play-by-play commentator and studio host. His
intimate knowledge of sports and timely sense of humor have
been demonstrated in his reportage of NBC Game-of-the-Week
in baseball, NFL football and college basketball games as well
as the pre-game shows during the 1984 World Series. While
most of the major sports events he covers do not qualify as
new products, some of the action, and the way he describes it
definitely are.

**2:30 p.m.**
Afternoon Session, Grand Ballroom
**New Product Review—1986**

**Martin J. Friedman,** Editor
DFS/Dorland Worldwide's **New
Product News**

Marty spent 15 years with DFS, moving from Associate
Director of Merchandising to Senior Vice President. Although
he retired in 1974, he continues to write **New Product News**
and acts as a consultant in promotion, marketing and new
products. His presentation highlights the new food and drug
products launched during the past year, covers trends in
consumer buying habits and future trends in new product
activity. Included among the trends he sees are an upgrading
of food products and more sophisticated test marketing
methods.

**Win, Place or Show: Retailers Rate
New Product Entries**
A panel discussion moderated by **Martin J. Friedman**

Panelists: **Robert M. Costello,** Director of Grocery
and Frozen Food Operations
D'Agostino Supermarkets

**Randell Deuser,** Director of Merchandising
J.M. Jones Company
Division of Super Valu Stores, Inc.

**Brooke Lennon,** Vice President, Grocery
Merchandising
Grand Union Company

**Stanley S. Sorkin,** Director of Purchasing,
Frozen & Grocery
Pathmark Division,
Supermarkets General Corporation

The panelists will review a dozen new products, give them
a "thumbs-up" or "thumbs down", and explain why they
feel these products would or would not be successful in their
outlets.

**4:00 p.m.**
**Prize Drawing and Adjournment**

---

Reprinted courtesy of American Association of National Advertisers.

Figure 2.   American Management Association Agenda for New Product Development
Courses, 1987

# NEW PRODUCT
# DEVELOPMENT

## PLANNING AND DEVELOPING NEW PRODUCTS AND MARKETS — 5576G87

**Map out all the critical elements you need to launch a
new product . . . or create a viable new market**

This course is designed for all those involved in new
product decisions: Marketing Vice Presidents and
Managers, Product Managers, Managers of New Product
Development, Managers of Product Planning and
Corporate Planning Executives, R&D Directors and
Managers, and specialists involved in new product
design.

**KEY TOPICS:**

■ Determining if new products are in line with overall
corporate strategy

■ How to direct, manage, and control creativity

■ How to use market research to target your market

■ Preliminary screening—telling the difference between
a good idea and a better one

■ Ways to develop markets and marketing strategies for
new products

■ Developing a business proposal to analyze the profit
potential of new products

■ The team approach to managing new products and
markets

**4 DAYS/2.5 CEU AWARDED**
**AMA MEMBERS $875; NONMEMBERS $975**

| 5576G87-19 | Jan. 26–29 | New York |
| 5576G87-20 | Feb. 17–20 | San Francisco |
| 5576G87-21 | Mar. 16–19 | Chicago |
| 5576G87-22 | Apr. 21–24 | Boston |
| 5576G87-25 | May 4–7 | Newport Beach, CA |
| 5576G87-23 | May 11–14 | Atlanta |
| 5576G87-26 | June 1–4 | Denver |
| 5576G87-24 | June 15–18 | Chicago |
| 5576G87-27 | July 20–23 | New York |
| 5576G87-30 | Aug. 10–13 | San Francisco |
| 5576G87-28 | Sept. 14–17 | Chicago |
| 5576G87-29 | Sept. 14–17 | Boston |
| 5576G87-31 | Oct. 19–22 | Atlanta |

## HOW TO CREATE NEW PRODUCTS — 5253G87

A course designed for Marketing Vice Presidents and
Managers, Product Managers, Managers of New Product
Development, Managers of Product Planning, and
Corporate Planning Executives, as well as R&D
specialists involved in new product planning.

**KEY TOPICS:**

■ Setting your company's needs for new products—a
new product/service strategy is formed by viewing how
customers, competitors, and your own company impact
on each other

■ Creative phase—techniques for using the creative
power of the technical, marketing, and manufacturing
people in your company

■ Implementation phase—techniques for getting new
products/services into the market

**SPECIAL FEATURE:**

**Creative workshops** in new product concepts to be
selected by registrants.

**2½ DAYS/1.5 CEU AWARDED**
**AMA MEMBERS $725; NONMEMBERS $830**

| 5253G87-13 | Apr. 1–3 | Chicago |
| 5253G87-14 | May 6–8 | New York |
| 5253G87-11 | Oct. | Chicago |

## LICENSING AND ACQUIRING NEW PRODUCTS AND TECHNOLOGY — 7220G87

This comprehensive program prepares you to develop
profitable licenses, negotiate affordable acquisitions, and
protect yourself every step of the way. It is specifically
designed for Presidents; Vice Presidents of Marketing,
Manufacturing, and R&D; Patent Counselors; General
Counselors; R&D Managers; and other key personnel
involved in licensing.

**KEY TOPICS:**

■ Principles and objectives of licensing

■ How to determine royalties

■ How to analyze a license agreement

■ How to negotiate the most favorable transaction

■ Trade secrets and know-how licensing

■ How to protect confidential information

■ Antitrust principles applied to licensing

■ Obtaining access to university-based technology

■ Licensing overseas technology

**2½ DAYS/1.5 CEU AWARDED**
**AMA MEMBERS $725; NONMEMBERS $830**

| 7220G87-70 | May 4–6 | Chicago |
| 7220G87-71 | June 8–10 | New York |
| 7220G87-72 | Oct. 14–16 | Chicago |

flecting the mind set of their association members—the national boundary focus of new product development for most U.S. companies.

Any attention paid by U.S. companies to international new products has been primarily (1) to follow the success of those which had been introduced into the U.S. market, or (2) to use introductions overseas as a source of ideas that might be copied domestically.

Foreign new products as a source for new product ideas was the major thrust of the World New Product Conference in Toronto which is outlined in figure 3. It is interesting to note that this world conference was held in Canada and not the United States. As the advertisement for the conference promises, marketers can "gain 20 years' experience in 2 days. In two days you can touch over 2,500 new products—or 20 times more than an average marketer touches in one year. . . . You'll encounter a wealth of ideas. Proven ideas that can start you working in a dozen profitable directions. Ideas that can give your company the competitive edge in tapping new products opportunities for growth."

A survey conducted during the conference showed that while 86 percent of the 421 respondents said overseas seemed to be a good source of new product ideas, the majority had done little to implement "any systematic approach to seek out new products concepts in foreign markets."[4]

Marketing Intelligence Service Ltd. is typical of a new kind of services being offered to U.S. companies for monitoring foreign new product activity (fig. 4). They promise, "If your company is among the nine out of ten that does not have an international new product intelligence service in place, contact [us]. . . . The chances are excellent that we will be able to reduce significantly the losses associated with new product failures and increase the odds of new product success." So here, even in the area of international new product intelligence, the major application is domestic in nature.

In addition, U.S. companies have tended to do a poor job even within their own multinational network to make the most of foreign innovation. Robert Ronstadt and Robert Kramer pointed this out in their article "Getting the Most out of Innovation Abroad." Their conclusion was that although many American multinational corporations have access to overseas research and development, they have infrequently utilized these resources to produce major technological innovations. As a result, the once dominant position of the U.S. in many markets continues to erode. Ronstadt and Kramer's study highlighted the weak international innovation efforts made by U.S. firms and suggested various ways to capitalize on existing resources.[5]

It appears that a national boundary phobia plagues most new product development programs today. Based on the current attitudes and actions, therefore, it would seem that for new product development in most U.S. consumer goods companies the utilization of Levitt's globalization concept will be a long way off.

Figure 3.   World New Products Conference Advertisement

Reprinted courtesy of Product Initiatives.

Figure 4. Marketing Intelligence Service Ltd. Advertisement

# If your company is engaged in new product development, we can help save you millions of dollars, months of research and improve the odds for successful new product introductions

Reprinted courtesy of Marketing Intelligence Service Ltd.

## How Globalization Might Change the Current New Product Development Process

The task of globalization could be a formidable one when you consider the new product development programs that seem to be in place in the majority of U.S. consumer goods companies. The following sections highlight some examples of the type of modifications that might have to be made at each step of the process. Table 4 summarizes these changes based on a composite of the Stephen King and Booz, Allen new product models.

### Examples of Changes in the Planning Stage

First and most important, the strategic objectives for the company would have to establish globalization as a major goal. Obviously, the whole global thrust of the program would have to be endorsed by top management as a part of long-term strategic planning.

In reviewing *company assets and capabilities,* the entire international scope of the company would have to be considered. For example, this would call for an appraisal of worldwide production facilities including any special know-how or technology, unused capacity, seasonal production opportunities, existing patents, special raw material positions worldwide. It would call for a review of current distribution facilities worldwide including any goodwill or special know-how. The global talent pool of marketing/sales people would have to be evaluated—special global know-how itself would be a particularly valuable people asset. Worldwide consumer brand names and franchises would need to be evaluated. An appraisal would have to be made of the company's worldwide financial requirements—new product investment capabilities as well as payout, volume, and margin requirements.

To establish a *technical innovation policy,* a review would have to be made of worldwide existing or potential research and development (R&D) capabilities. Based on this appraisal plus objects/costs, an R&D global policy would have to be established. The coordination of R&D on a worldwide basis would be critical.

In the search for *product categories* to develop, the critical need would be to obtain standardized consumer research information on an international basis. A cluster analysis of countries by market size, penetration, and demographics for each category would be important.

In establishing a *global new product policy,* it would be essential to develop a priority list for entering each country by product category. It would also be important to set up a policy on local versus regional versus multinational versus global brands.

Table 4.   How Globalization Could Affect Different Steps in Current
U.S. New Product Development Programs

### Planning Stage

| Current U.S. New Product Development Programs | Possible Changes or Additions Indicated by Globalization |
|---|---|
| 1. Strategic planning and analysis of company assets. | 1. Establish global objectives: Review company assets on a global basis. |
| 2. Evaluate R&D capability and policy. | 2. Establish global R&D policy. |
| 3. Search for product categories. | 3. Perform cluster analysis of countries by key demographics for each product category. |
| 4. New product policy:<br>A. Objectives<br>B. R&D policy<br>C. Product categories to be explored<br>D. Financial requirements | 4. Establish a **global new product policy**. Include priority list for entering each country by product category. Set up guidelines for regional vs. worldwide brands. |
| 5. Research on consumers and consumption. | 5. Critical to review attitudes and usage by category in at least top priority countries. Be aware of any major attitude/usage differences by country. |
| 6. Review of current technology. | 6. Be aware of technological progress worldwide. |
| 7. Idea generation. | 7. Encourage idea generation in key countries. |
| 8. Concept development and research. | 8. Include at least top priority countries in focus groups and other concept research. Look for strong, motivating concepts that don't depend on provincial executional devices. |

### Development Stage

| | |
|---|---|
| 9. Creative strategy for winning concept[s]. | 9. Utilize people with global viewpoint and knowledge to develop final creative strategy. |
| 10. Develop physical product. | 10. Check legal differences on ingredients. Assess ingredient cost/availability differences globally. |

Table 4. (continued)

| Current U.S. New Product Development Programs | Possible Changes or Additions Indicated by Globalization |
|---|---|
| 11. Develop communications:<br>A. Positioning<br>B. Packaging<br><br>C. Brand name<br><br><br><br><br><br>D. Advertising | 11. **Positioning.** Avoid provincial, fadish, short-term positionings.<br>**Packaging.** Be aware of global differences in form/sizing/pricing. Need strong unifying graphic design.<br>**Brand name.** Coined names and names with universal visual symbols will be better globally. Names that "sound out" the same in any language are good. Avoid names that translate poorly. Protect name legally on global basis.<br>**Advertising.** Strong visual symbols and demos good. Avoid idioms and plays on words. Music universal. Work in media common to cluster group-- usually print and TV/movie theater. Buy talent, music, artwork with global options. |
| 12. Preliminary product tests. | 12. Include key countries. |
| 13. Preliminary communications tests. | 13. Include key countries. |
| 14. Initial prototype brand tests combining product and communications. | 14. Set up prototype brand tests on global basis. |

## Evaluation Stage

| | |
|---|---|
| 15. Production development. | 15. Work out global production plan. Be sure key production units are part of production development process. |
| 16. Final packaging/advertising and testing. | 16. Include key countries in test pattern. |
| 17. Quantitative laboratory pretest. | 17. Include key priority countries in sample. |
| 18. Production planning and costing. | 18. Work out process and costs for each area included in global production plan. Try to minimize production, size and price differences. |
| 19. Marketing plan and implementation. | 19. Include global rollout plan. |
| 20. Test marketing: full, mini, standardized service. | 20. Include key priority countries in sample. |

In *researching consumers and consumption,* it would be critical to review attitudes and usage by category in at least the top priority countries. There would be a need for broad, motivating common denominators—a need to be aware of the major attitude/usage similarities and differences by country.

In reviewing *current technology,* it would be essential to be as aware as possible of technological progress worldwide for the category. *Idea generation* should be encouraged on a worldwide basis taking advantage of groups and facilities available to the company globally.

*Concept development and research* should include focus groups and other exploratory research in at least the top priority countries. It would be key to look for strong, basic, motivating concepts that do not depend on provincial images and ideas.

## Examples of Changes in the Development Stage

It would be essential that the final *creative strategy* for each concept was approved by new product team members who have a thorough knowledge of the key world areas on the product's priority list. It would be essential to avoid positionings which are not broad, basic motivators.

In *developing the physical product,* it would be important to check legal differences on ingredient requirements by country, assess ingredient cost/availability differences globally, and look for special advantages in raw material procurement which may exist in particular countries.

In *developing the communications,* the best *brand names* would be those that sound the same in any language and that minimize translation problems. Coined words (Kodak, Coke) would tend to be good, as would those that suggest universal visual symbols (Shell, Camel). It would be important to set up a system to protect names internationally.

*Packaging* would need to incorporate a strong unifying and universal visual design. There should be a disciplined attempt to minimize differences in form/sizing/pricing country by country. It would be important to be aware of legal differences on packaging requirements country by country.

*Advertising* with strong, universal, visual symbols and demonstrations would be good—avoiding local idioms and play on word expressions. Imagery with minimal copy would work well. Music could be universal. Caution should be used when considering humor, which is often not universal. Creative work should be done for media common to top priority countries—usually print and TV/movie theatre. Legal restrictions country by country would have to be taken into account. It would be efficient to shoot commercials at one time in different languages. Music, talent, artwork, and photography should be bought with worldwide options.

For *preliminary product tests, communication tests, and initial prototype brand tests,* it would be essential to include a sample from at least the key priority countries.

### Examples of Change in the Evaluation and Commercialization Stage

For *production development,* it would be important to work out a global production plan making certain that all key production units are considered for the mass production process. *Final packaging and advertising tests* should include a sample from at least the key priority countries.

For *production planning and costing,* work should be done on the basis of the global production plan. It would be key to standardize production, product forms, sizes, and pricing as much as possible.

The *marketing plan and its implementation* should include a global rollout plan or, if called for, a worldwide introduction plan. Whatever form of *test marketing* is used, it would be important to include a representative sample from at least the top priority countries.

### Examples of Change in Staffing, Organization and Control

As Michael Porter has stressed in his book, *Competition in Global Industries,* "today's game of global strategy seems increasingly to be a game of coordination. . . . Successful international competitors in the future will be those who can seek out competitive advantages from global configuration/coordination anywhere in the value chain, and overcome the organizational barriers to exploiting them."[6]

There is no doubt that expert coordination is absolutely critical for successful global new product development. First, the coordination of an international network on new product intelligence will be essential. Global expansion with new innovation simply cannot take place in a vacuum and requires the latest information and knowledge about changing markets, new introductions, and current category trends in each country.

Second, the coordination of the new product activity must be staffed by a whole new breed of globally oriented marketing people—a group that will undoubtedly be in short supply. The organization will have to transcend national boundaries using the best staff the company had on a world basis. It will be a very difficult human relations problem—getting people worldwide to input ideas up-front, getting people to feel they are a part of the final global policy, and, when the product is launched, getting them to minimize local adaptation.

It is clear that globalization of new product development will be more expensive and time consuming than the practice now believed to exist. These programs will also require considerably talented managers—people who are innovative and yet possess a knowledgeable, global viewpoint. Most importantly, these programs will require the involvement and direction of a top management which is firmly committed to the globalization of markets; a top management which looks at long-term planning with a firm conviction that Theodore Levitt is right—"Companies that do not adapt to the new global realities will become victims of those that do"[7]—a top management which will no longer tolerate new product development on a national boundary basis.

Even with full acceptance of global new product development as a strategy, successful implementation is not easy. The implementation issue is so critical that chapter 7 is devoted to a more complete discussion of this subject.

# 5

# How Three Global Companies Handle New Products for a World Market

## Rickitt & Coleman

Rickitt & Coleman is a highly successful British consumer goods company operating in more than 45 different countries and dealing in a large array of food and household products. The company is a world leader in household starches, air fresheners, window cleaners, and bathroom cleaning supplies as well as mustards and other specialty foods. In the U.S., Rickitt's most familiar brand names are French's, Durkee, and Airwick.

Rickitt has developed over the years a fine-tuned system of global coordination, communication, and control—particularly in the area of new product development. The coordinating group for new product development is a special unit within corporate planning called the International Development Department—known in the company as IDD. This strategic group acts, in effect, as the parent organization's central intelligence center and think tank. IDD keeps in constant touch with Rickitt product management and R&D people around the world.

There are several things about IDD that are important to note. First, it is a staff group with no line authority. Second, it comprises a small select group of four to five seasoned marketing executives who report directly to the vice president-group director of corporate planning. Importantly, this vice president is one of the most prominent members of the Rickitt board of directors. Third, IDD is looked upon by the rest of the company as an elite group and one in which it would be an honor to serve. The staffing of IDD changes from time to time. Many group product managers in the company have served on IDD, and from that position have moved on to higher levels throughout the organization worldwide.

The function of IDD is to collect and present information on all the key product categories in which the company is involved worldwide. Once each quarter, IDD issues a written review for each important product category in which the company competes. This review is sent to all the key marketing and

R&D people worldwide who are involved with the category. The report includes such information as world category sales, leading manufacturers brands and shares worldwide, important trends on a global basis as well as in specific countries, and important new product tests and introductions—both Rickitt's and competitors—country by country.

Members of IDD travel extensively to meet with brand management and R&D people in each country—the purpose being to gain and exchange information. Once a year there is a two-to-three-day IDD conference for each key product category. This is intentionally held in a different country each year so that Rickitt people will be exposed firsthand to a different market. The conference is attended by at least one representative of each product group for the category from every country around the world. Key R&D people for the particular category also attend. The purpose is to gain and exchange information on the category involved. These conferences often produce a consensus about key product trends and common goals that should be achieved for the future.

In the area of new products, this information network is invaluable. For example, IDD may report the introduction or testing of a new product by a competitor in a specific country. Sometimes IDD might make a projection of just what countries will be next on the competitors rollout list. Cases of this new product are automatically sent out to product managers throughout the world for inspection and study. This kind of information has made it possible to introduce a countering Rickitt product into a country before the competitor has a chance to rollout. A strategy may even evolve from this information that calls for a timetable of Rickett new product introductions in the category country by country.

Another interesting type of new product information from IDD has been trend information. For example, IDD may project that a definite trend toward a new product form is underway in many countries. With this knowledge, product managers can plan ahead and watch for this trend in their own specific area.

IDD also expedites new product introductions by providing information on formulas, patents, and packaging that might be used. It is interesting to note that on the basis of an IDD recommendation, Rickitt will provide a special fund to launch a product or line of products in a specific country where financing the introduction may not be possible on the basis of local sales.

It should be pointed out that Rickitt does not force a completely standardized approach worldwide for a new product but does allow for local customization of those marketing elements which may need adaptation. Through the constant contact with, and input of, IDD, many of the normal "not invented here" problems do not emerge.

As previously mentioned, IDD is a staff function with no line authority. Yet, marketing people in the company have such respect for the work of IDD that in most all cases they follow IDD's advice and guidance. For a product manager in a specific country, IDD exposure is a frequent and necessary part of the job—exposure through either the category review published quarterly, the personal visits from IDD staff members, or attendance at the annual worldwide category conference.

There is little doubt that Rickitt & Coleman's International Development Department is an excellent example of the quality of coordination and implementation of strategy that is needed to deal with new product development on a world basis.

## International Business Machines

International Business Machines (IBM) is probably the best example of a U.S.-based multinational company engaged in global new product development. Ever since the mid-1950s the company has been involved with a world plan for product development that is carefully stressed in the mission and scope statements for each division. Today national product treatments are a very small part of IBM's business.

The key ingredient of this process is a worldwide intelligence system and fine-tuned coordination between local and headquarters people. The key coordination group for new product development is the Worldwide Product Development Group. This is an R&D-oriented staff based in the U.S. which is responsible for all new product introductions worldwide. Because of the high tech nature of the product, this group works eight years ahead of actual introduction date. Its prime responsibility is to coordinate the new product activity and encourage an exchange and input of information from IBM's local business area organizations around the world.

A healthy give and take exchange is frequent between the Worldwide Product Development Group and the various business area organizations. This involves frequent personal meetings as well as constant written communication. There are two formal coordination meetings each year that bring the entire organization together. At the spring meeting the local business areas must forecast their market needs for at least eight years ahead. New products by functions are then reviewed for the long term. The Worldwide Product Development Group is told what is good and bad about projected new products for each area. These are very frank meetings with a great deal of give and take.

The second meeting of the year is a short- and long-term budget type of meeting during which agreement must be reached between the two groups on the specific long-term new product projects to be pursued. The key issues of both these meetings are to make certain that the world product will be right for each business area, that the cost of development is feasible, and that the final costs of production will be in keeping with expected financial goals. Understanding the market requirements for each area and making certain these needs are reflected in the global new product development plan is critical.

Throughout the process market "intelligence" is critical. This comes from people inside and outside of the organization; it comes from the grass roots up and from the top down. Government information is used, outside research is purchased, and primary research may be conducted.

It should be pointed out that the IBM system is global to the extent of development of a world product. Other parts of the marketing mix may be adapted locally. The real objective of the program is a standard, superior product that can be successfully introduced worldwide, not a standard marketing program.

The system of coordination is complex, expensive, and time consuming. It requires the right people with the skill and know-how to make it work. It has taken IBM many years to perfect. Without question, it represents one of the most superior methods of global new product development in operation anywhere today.

## Colgate-Palmolive

For some time now Colgate-Palmolive has been a leader in adapting a global marketing strategy which standardizes as many parts of the marketing mix as is feasible. With this strategy has also come an evolving organization to handle marketing on a global basis.

Although new product activity still exists at both the global level and the foreign subsidiary level, there has been a move toward more and more global new product development. The key coordinating unit for global new product development is the Business Development Group located at headquarters in New York. This group consists of highly experienced, seasoned marketing executives, all of whom have come up through international marketing channels.

The Business Development Group has as its responsibility the assessment of new markets, new categories, new areas worldwide in which Colgate should invest time and effort. It also serves as an intelligence center for market information and competitive product and category trends worldwide. The Business Development Group really acts as the "marketing director" of the company. It is the key coordinating group in all marketing areas, including new products.

Colgate has established specific executives to coordinate very specific areas of the marketing mix. For example, there is a global advertising director whose responsibility it is to coordinate advertising worldwide. A great deal has been done to extend successful benchmark campaigns to many countries with minimum local adaptation. With increasing emphasis on global new products, it is anticipated that further organizational changes will be made to globalize the new product function even further.

Now that we have looked at how three globally oriented companies have successfully handled the new product function, let us consider how the majority of the U.S. multinational consumer goods companies handle new products. We will find out what consumer goods marketers actually think about global new product development, its value to them, and the feasibility of executing such a strategy.

# 6

# How Most U.S. Multinational Consumer Goods Companies Handle New Products

In 1985 a major research study was completed among the 137 leading U.S.-based multinational consumer goods companies. The principle objective of this study was to validate my belief that:

1. The globalization of markets concept is being utilized by increasing numbers of U.S.-based multinational consumer goods companies on *existing* products.
2. Globalization is *not* being adopted by U.S.-based multinational consumer goods companies for *new* product development—the key area for future expansion.
3. To implement global new product development, U.S.-based multinational consumer goods companies would require major changes in their current new product programs—changes in philosophy, methodology, and organization.

It was also our purpose to describe and analyze the current new product development process in U.S. multinational consumer goods companies and to identify whether these companies had a *global* or *local* focus. Emphasis was placed on questions in three critical areas:

*Philosophy and strategy:* What was the geographic focus of the new product development program? Was there a current recognition of the need for the global acceptance of new products now being developed? Was globalization a part of the company's long-term strategy?

*Organization and structure:* How was the company's new product development program currently structured? Was it corporate or divisional? Were international marketing personnel a part of the structure?

*Methodology and process:* What was the new product development process currently followed? Was globalization incorporated in any way into the planning, development or evaluation process?

In my research I employed a descriptive study utilizing a mail survey plus selective personal interviews. All data collection was based on a structured questionnaire that combined factual information and attitudinal responses. Initially the questionnaire was mailed to the presidents of the companies in the sample. When necessary to complete the sample, other top executives were contacted.

For the purpose of this study, consumer goods and services are defined as frequently purchased, advertised, and promoted products such as food, beverages, cigarettes, proprietary drugs, toiletries, cosmetics, fragrances, etc. Not included are heavy goods, automobiles, and agricultural, industrial, or high tech products.

The sample was drawn from all the U.S. companies that sell consumer goods and services internationally and have substantial direct capital investments in foreign markets. The specific sample frame was all U.S. consumer goods companies listed in the *Directory of American Firms Operating in Foreign Countries.*[1] It should be noted that the directory list is overwhelmingly high tech, industrial, and agricultural. The consumer goods companies selected for the sample, therefore, were the entire universe of consumer goods companies listed in the directory.

This list was cross-checked and ranked in order of importance using two additional sources: *Forbes'* list of the 125 largest U.S. multinational companies;[2] and *Advertising Age's* top 100 leading advertisers.[3]

The 58 companies which ranked highest in terms of size and advertising expenditures are show in table 5. The remaining 79 companies from our survey universe sample are listed in table 6.

The sample unit from each company was selected on the basis of this priority:

1. President.
2. Top corporate executive whose direct responsibility includes new product development.
3. New product directors.
4. Marketing Director whose duties cover both existing and new products.
5. New product brand managers.
6. Brand management.

Screening for the correct individual to be contacted in each company was based on published sources, available listings of company executives, and exploratory telephone calls directly to the companies involved.

The questionnaire was pretested by a select group of company presidents. These executives were asked to comment on anything that was unclear, confusing, or not explicit enough to answer accurately. After the pretest, modifications were made to the questionnaire and it was mailed to the total sample.

# Table 5. The 58 Leading U.S. Consumer Product/Services Companies Selling Internationally

| | Rank as Top U.S. Multinational[1] | Rank as Top U.S. Advertisers[2] | Principal Consumer Business[3] |
|---|---|---|---|
| 1. Proctor and Gamble | 21 | 1 | Soaps, toiletries, paper products, food |
| 2. Eastman Kodak | 24 | 47 | Film, cameras |
| 3. Union Carbide | 30 | 73 | Batteries |
| 4. Dart & Kraft | 31 | 30 | Food |
| 5. Coca-Cola | 32 | 22 | Soft drinks, food |
| 6. Colgate-Palmolive | 34 | 24 | Soap, toiletries, household products |
| 7. CPC International | 35 | 71 | Food |
| 8. American Express | 36 | 66 | Credit cards |
| 9. Johnson & Johnson | 40 | 17 | First aid, toiletries, personal products |
| 10. Nabisco Brands | 41 | 11 | Food |
| 11. Beatrice Foods | 45 | 3 | Food |
| 12. American Brands | 46 | 79 | Cigarettes, toiletries |
| 13. Pfizer | 50 | 83 | Drugs |
| 14. General Foods | 54 | 10 | Food |
| 15. R. J. Reynolds Industries | 63 | 5 | Cigarettes, food |
| 16. Consolidated Foods | 70 | 33 | Food |
| 17. Merck | 71 | — | Drugs |
| 18. American Home Products | 73 | 14 | Drugs, food, households |
| 19. H. J. Heinz | 74 | 31 | Food |

## Table 5. (continued)

| | | Rank as Top U.S. Multinational[1] | Rank as Top U.S. Advertisers[2] | Principal Consumer Business[3] |
|---|---|---|---|---|
| 20. | Warner-Lambert | 75 | 13 | Drugs, toiletries |
| 21. | Bristol-Myers | 77 | 26 | Drugs, toiletries |
| 22. | Scott Paper | 79 | — | Paper products |
| 23. | PepsiCo | 80 | 12 | Beverages |
| 24. | Philip Morris | 82 | 6 | Cigarettes, beverages |
| 25. | Gillette | 83 | 35 | Shaving products, toiletries |
| 26. | American Cyanamid | 85 | 45 | Toiletries, cosmetics |
| 27. | Avon Products | 88 | — | Cosmetics, toiletries |
| 28. | Kimberly-Clark | 91 | 77 | Paper products |
| 29. | Eli Lilly | 93 | — | Drugs |
| 30. | Ralston Purina | 94 | 21 | Food |
| 31. | Smithkline Beckman | 95 | — | Drugs |
| 32. | Quaker Oats | 98 | 42 | Food |
| 33. | Carnation | 100 | 99 | Food |
| 34. | Schering-Plough | 110 | 59 | Drugs, toiletries |
| 35. | Kellogg | 112 | 37 | Food |
| 36. | Abbott Laboratories | 113 | — | Drugs |
| 37. | Borden | 118 | — | Food |
| 38. | Squibb | 120 | — | Drugs |
| 39. | Revlon, Inc. | 124 | 53 | Cosmetics |

| | Rank as Top U.S. Multinational[1] | Rank as Top U.S. Advertisers[2] | Principal Consumer Business[3] |
|---|---|---|---|
| 40. McDonald's | — | 26 | Fast food |
| 41. Anheuser-Busch | — | 20 | Beer |
| 42. General Mills | — | 23 | Food |
| 43. Pillsbury | — | 34 | Food |
| 44. Mattel, Inc. | — | 36 | Toys |
| 45. Sterling Drug | — | 38 | Drugs |
| 46. Richardson-Vicks | — | 41 | Drugs, toiletries |
| 47. Chesebrough-Pond's | — | 46 | Cosmetics, toiletries |
| 48. Campbell Soup Company | — | 52 | Food |
| 49. Mars, Inc. | — | 55 | Confections |
| 50. Miles Laboratories | — | 72 | Drugs |
| 51. S. C. Johnson & Company | — | 74 | Household products |
| 52. Stroh Brewery Company | — | 82 | Beer |
| 53. Clorox Company | — | 88 | Household products |
| 54. Hershey Foods Corp. | — | 89 | Food, chocolate |
| 55. Wendy's International | — | 90 | Fast food |
| 56. Wm. Wrigley Jr. Co. | — | 91 | Confections |
| 57. Adolph Coors Company | — | 93 | Beer |
| 58. Noxell Corporation | — | 94 | Cosmetics, toiletries |

Sources:
1. "The 125 Largest U.S. Multinational Companies," *Forbes* (July 2, 1984), p. 129.
2. "Top 100 Leading Advertisers," *Advertising Age* (September 14, 1984), p. 1.
3. *Directory of American Firms Operating in Foreign Countries*, Uniworld Business Publications, 1984.

Table 6.   The Remaining 79 Consumer Goods Companies Listed in the
*Directory of American Firms Operating in Foreign Countries*

| | |
|---|---|
| Alberto-Culver Company | IC Industries |
| Allergan Pharmaceuticals Int'l. | Ideal Toy Corp. |
| American Greeting Corporation | ITT Continental Baking Co. |
| Amway Corporation | Kolmar Laboratories, Inc. |
| Anderson Clayton | Lehn and Fink |
| Avis Rent Car System, Inc. | Levi Strauss & Co. |
| Bausch & Lomb, Inc. | Mary Kay Cosmetics |
| Baxter Travenol Laboratories, Inc. | Mennen Co. |
| Black & Decker Mfg. Co. | Mentholatum Co. |
| H & R Block, Inc. | Merle Norman Cosmetics |
| Blue Bell, Inc. | Milton Bradley Co. |
| Brillo Manufacturing Co. | National Car Rental |
| Brown-Forman Distillers Corp. | National Distillers |
| Burger King Corp. | Norcliff-Thayer |
| Calgon Corp. | Northrup King & Co. |
| Canada Dry Int'l Corp. | Norwich-Eaton |
| Carter-Wallace, Inc. | Parke-Davis |
| Castle and Cooke | Parker Pen Co. |
| CBS Records Group DIV CBS | Pet, Inc. |
| Charles of the Ritz, Ltd. | Pizza Hut, Inc. |
| Church & Dwight Co., Inc. | Polaroid Corp. |
| Cooper Laboratories | Purex Industries |
| Di Giorgio Corp. | Reader's Digest Assoc. |
| Diner's Club | Redken Laboratories |
| Dow Chemical Co. | Schenley Industries |
| Dr. Pepper Co. | Scripto, Inc. |
| Dunkin' Donuts of America, Inc. | G. D. Searle & Co. |
| Economics Laboratory, Inc. | Sheaffer Eaton |
| Elizabeth Arden, Inc. | Stokely-Van Camp, Inc. |
| Estee Lauder Int'l., Inc. | Tambrands |
| Ex-Lax Pharmaceutical Co., Inc. | 3M Company |
| Fisher Price Toys | Time, Inc. |
| Fleer Corp. | Tupperware Mfg. Co. |
| Franklin Mint Corp. | Wm. Underwood Co. |
| Gerber Products Co. | United Brands Co. |
| Hasbro Industries, Inc. | Universal Foods Corp. |
| Helena Rubinstein | Upjohn Co. |
| Helene Curtis Industries, Inc. | J. B. Williams |
| Hertz Int'l., Ltd. | Wilson Foods Corp. |

Source: *Directory of American Firms Operating in Foreign Countries*, Uniworld Business Publications, 1984.

The 72 executives who responded for the study represented 36 percent of the total sample universe (137 leading U.S. consumer goods companies now selling internationally plus 63 divisions and subsidiaries). The sample represented an excellent range of both food and nonfood consumer product categories.

A senior management viewpoint emerged since of the sample respondents, 14 were chairmen or presidents; 10 were executive, corporate, or senior vice presidents; 39 were vice presidents; and 7 were middle management executives. This also represented a highly seasoned group in new product development— 52 out of 72 had been involved in new product development for more than 10 years. (See tables 7 and 8.)

Table 7.   Breakdown of Sample Responding

|  |  |  | Total Executives |
|---|---|---|---|
| **Nonfood** | | | 38 |
| | cigarettes, tobacco | 2 | |
| | conglomerates | 6 | |
| | cosmetics, fragrances | 3 | |
| | hair care, shaving preparations, razors/blades | 2 | |
| | household products, soap, detergents, toothpaste | 3 | |
| | paper, sanitary products, first aid | 5 | |
| | pharmaceuticals, proprietary drugs | 8 | |
| | writing materials | 2 | |
| | other | 7 | |
| **Food** | | | 34 |
| | beverages | 4 | |
| | confections, gum | 2 | |
| | fast foods | 3 | |
| | food products | 25 | |
| **Total** | | | 72 |

## What the Study Showed

The appendix provides the complete question-by-question results of the global new product development study. Following is a review of the findings related to key issues.

### Globalization of Existing Products

As a first step toward globalization, have many companies actually adopted the globalization strategy for their existing products?

It is one thing to globalize high tech, agricultural, or industrial products which have more universal appeal. It is quite another to globalize consumer goods where cultural differences in taste, values, and lifestyle are more dominant factors in the consumer purchase decision.

Table 8.   Information on the Respondents to Research Project

**Title of Executive Responding**

| | Total |
|---|---|
| Chairman | 2 |
| President | 12 |
| Executive, Corporate, or Senior Vice President | 10 |
| Vice President of Business Planning, Corporate Development, Business Development, Strategic Planning | 12 |
| Vice President of Marketing | 10 |
| Vice President and New Products Director | 9 |
| Vice President | 8 |
| Product Manager | 5 |
| Marketing Research Director | 2 |
| No answer | 2 |
| Total | 72 |

**Length of Time Executives Had Been Involved with New Product Development**

| | Years Involved |
|---|---|
| Over 10 years | 52 |
| 5 to 10 years | 13 |
| 3 to 4 years | 4 |
| 1 to 2 years | 2 |
| Less than 1 year | 1 |
| Not involved | 0 |
| Total Executives | 72 |

The study indicated that U.S. consumer goods companies were, indeed, involved in globalization. Nonfood companies in particular had moved strongly in that direction. About 61 percent of the nonfood companies (23 out of 38) stated that "with existing brands, they were looking toward a universal global strategy and, as much as possible, trying to keep all parts of the mix essentially the same in each country."

The 23 nonfood companies were involved with a wide range of existing products for globalization. For example:

| | |
|---|---|
| baby care | perfumes |
| bar soaps | personal products |
| bath products | pet products |
| batteries | pharmaceuticals |
| cigarettes | proprietary drugs |
| cosmetics | razors/blades |
| dental care | sanitary protection |
| face care | shaving preparations |
| film/cameras | small appliances/tools |
| first aid | tobacco products |
| foot care | toiletries — men |
| hair care | toiletries — women |
| hand lotion | toothpaste |
| household products | video tape |
| jeans, sports clothes | water softeners |
| laundry products | writing materials |
| paper products | |

The major hold-outs against globalization of existing products were the food companies (food, fast food, and beverages). Of 34 food companies, only 4 stated that they had adopted a globalization strategy on existing products. The food product categories involved for these four "globalized" food companies were:

> beverages
> breakfast foods
> confections
> chewing gum
> fast foods

This generally negative response among food companies was largely due to the belief that cultural differences in local foods and food tastes were too wide. While the research showed that U.S. food companies had not gone along with globalization, food executives' attitudes about the future were not all negative. When asked whether they felt globalization was a concept more and more companies would pursue, about half of the food executives agreed.

The data on the globalization of existing products for the total 72 companies responding in the study are summarized in table 9.

*Globalization of New Product Development*

The study showed that a relatively small number (11 percent) of U.S.-based multinational consumer goods companies were now following a global strategy

Table 9.    Globalization of Existing Products

|  | Nonfood | Food | Total |
|---|---|---|---|
| Have adopted a globalization strategy on existing products | 23 | 4 | 27 |
| Have not adopted a globalization policy on existing products | 15 | 29 | 44 |
| No answer | — | 1 | 1 |
| Total Companies | 38 | 34 | 72 |

Table 10.    New Product Development Policy for 72 U.S. Multinational Consumer Goods Companies

|  | Nonfood | Food | Total |
|---|---|---|---|
| New products are developed for the U.S. market and the successful products might later be sold internationally. | 7 | 8 | 15 |
| New products are developed both in the U.S. and by our foreign subsidiaries to be marketed in their own home country.  If successful, these products might later be expanded internationally. | 21 | 23 | 44 |
| New products are developed up front as global so that global considerations are built into the brand from the beginning. New products would usually be tested and introduced in more than one country from the start.  The new product would not be introduced unless it appeared to have viable sales potential globally. | 8 | — | 8 |
| No answer | 2 | 3 | 5 |
| Total Companies | 38 | 34 | 72 |

on new product development. As table 10 shows, none of the food companies were following the strategy; in the nonfood category a higher percentage (21 percent, or 8 of 38 companies) were involved with global new product development.

It appears, too, that "international involvement" in the new product process was not top-of-mind for most U.S. consumer goods executives. When asked which groups were deeply involved in the new product development process on a regular basis, out of 380 mentions, only 8 percent were "international marketing personnel." Or when discussing changes made in the last 12 months to improve the new product function, only one executive mentioned "improved international participation" as an improvement. Ninety-three percent of the executives said they were basically following the Booz, Allen model in their new product program which, as previously discussed, tends to be a home-country oriented model.

The study also indicated that globalization of markets tend to be a two step process:

Phase 1:    Globalization of existing brands
Phase 2:    Globalization of new products

In all cases where companies had established a global new product development process, the company had first adopted a global policy on existing products. Likewise, an even greater number of companies had globalized existing products but had not, as yet, adopted global new product development.

Table 11 shows that out of 27 companies who were in phase 1 (globalization of existing brands), 8 companies had moved to phase 2 (globalization of new products). These companies were all in the nonfood category.

The eight companies now in phase 2 were involved with a wide range of product categories:

| Company | Product Categories |
|---|---|
| A | cigarettes, tobacco products, beverages, food |
| B | personal products, sanitary protection, hair care products, cosmetics, perfume |
| C | writing materials |
| D | pharmaceuticals, proprietary drugs, cosmetics, foot care, toiletries, pet care |
| E | small appliances, small power tools |
| F | bath products, water softeners |
| G | film, cameras, video tape, batteries |
| H | bar soaps, laundry detergents, household products, hand lotion, toothpaste, first aid, shaving preparations |

It is also interesting to note that even among companies *not* adopting a global new product strategy, 22 percent said they would not proceed with a new product unless it *appeared to have viable potential beyond the United States* (table 12). The balance of the companies (88 percent) were U.S.-oriented in their geographic focus.

Table 11.  New Product Development Policy for 27 Companies
Already in Phase 1

|  | Nonfood | Food | Total |
|---|---|---|---|
| **Develop New Product for:** | | | |
| Global use (Phase 2 policy) | 8* | -- | 8 |
| Home country use for possible expansion later | 14* | 2 | 16 |
| U.S. market only for possible expansion later | 3 | 2 | 5 |
|  | 25* | 4 | 29 |
| Total Companies | 23 | 4 | 27 |

*Two companies have both global and home country development.

Table 12.  Geographic Focus for 64 Companies Not Practicing
Global New Product Development

|  | Nonfood | Food | Total |
|---|---|---|---|
| **Would Not Introduce a New Product Unless It Appeared to Have Viable Potential In:** | | | |
| Worldwide | 1 | -- | 1 |
| Any major world area | 2 | 2 | 4 |
| North America plus one major area | -- | 1 | 1 |
| North America | 1 | 1 | 2 |
| The U.S. plus at least one major country or area | 3 | 3 | 6 |
| Total Beyond the U.S. | 7 | 7 | 14 |
| The total U.S. | 16 | 13 | 29 |
| A major part of the U.S. | 8 | 13 | 21 |
| Total Companies | 31 | 33 | 64 |

The study clearly shows that global new product development is a concept in the very initial stages of acceptance. However, there is considerable belief among the executives studied that an increasing number of consumer goods companies, particularly nonfood companies, will adopt the concept in the future.

It is also evident that product category has a strong influence on whether or not companies globalize. Table 13 summarizes the global strategy on both existing and new products by specific product categories. Included, too, are executives' attitudes on globalization and its future. A good portion of the nonfood product categories studied were perceived by the companies involved as candidates for globalization. The reverse tended to be true for the food product category where only four companies had a global strategy on existing brands and none were global on new product development.

*Executive Attitudes about Global New Product Development*

Executives were asked their opinion of global new product development regardless of whether their company had adopted the concept. Two-thirds of the nonfood company executives had a positive attitude about global new product development. About half of these executives did have some reservations about implementation and adjustments that might have to be made to carry it out. Only 24 percent (8 of 34) of the food company executives had a positive attitude about the concept (see table 14).

*Highly positive attitudes.* Those company executives with a highly positive attitude toward global new product development advanced this type of reasoning:

1. It is a competitive necessity—competition is now global.
2. The market is now worldwide—it is no longer a national issue.
3. Consumers are becoming more similar worldwide which makes the concept possible.
4. It is necessary to leverage high new product costs—R&D, production, marketing expenses.

Typical highly positive comments:

Given the escalating cost of a major new product launch, it is increasingly important to develop global brands from the outset. Our competitors are so big, so strong, and so global themselves they will quickly exploit a new success in one country into many others. Naturally, the return is better if development costs can be shared over several countries at once. Our major product in the company has the same positioning and look around the world although details of the copy execution may vary some. *Nonfood*

Thinking of new products as global brands is the best option—particularly when the R&D and/or capital requirements are high. It allows you a high leverage on your investment and effort. *Nonfood*

## Table 13.  Summary of Policy and Attitudes on Globalization

| 38 Nonfood Companies by Product Types | Existing Products | |
|---|---|---|
| | Now Adopt Locally | Phase 1 Global |
| 1. Bar soaps, detergents, household, toothpaste | | x |
| 2. Bath products, water softeners | | x |
| 3. Cigarettes, tobacco products, beverages, food | | x |
| 4. Pharmaceuticals, proprietaries, cosmetics | | x |
| 5. Personal products, sanitary protection, hair, cosmetics | | x |
| 6. Writing materials | | x |
| 7. Small appliances/tools | | x |
| 8. Film, cameras, videotape, batteries | | x |
| 9. Razors, blades | | x |
| 10. Sanitary protection, household paper products | | x |
| 11. Proprietaries, pharmaceuticals, household, cosmetics, toiletries | | x |
| 12. Cosmetics, toiletries, perfumes, food, clothing | | x |
| 13. Batteries | | x |
| 14. Cosmetics, perfumes, nail care | | x |
| 15. First aid, toiletries, baby care, dental care | | x |
| 16. Proprietary drugs, skin care | | x |
| 17. Sanitary protection, personal products | | x |
| 18. Hair care, razors/blades, toiletries, shaving preps | | x |
| 19. Proprietary drugs, household products | | x |
| 20. Cosmetics, toiletries, proprietary drugs | | x |
| 21. Cigarettes, beverages, tobacco products | | x |
| 22. Proprietary drugs, toiletries, face care | x | x |
| 23. Jeans, sports clothing | | x |
| 24. Cosmetics, toiletries, fragrances, jewelry | x | |
| 25. Toiletries, health/beauty aids | x | |

| New Products | | | Positive Attitudes on Global New Product Development | | | |
|---|---|---|---|---|---|---|
| U.S. Development Only | Home Country Development | Phase 2 Global New Products | Positive | Essential for Future | Feasible and Practical | More Companies Will Do |
|  | x | x[a] | x | x | x | x |
|  |  | x | x | x | x | x |
|  | x | x[a] | x | x | x | x |
|  |  | x | x | x | x | x |
|  |  | x | x | x | x | x |
|  |  | x | x | x | x | x |
|  |  | x | x | x | x | x |
|  |  | x | x | x | x | x |
|  | x |  | x | x | x | x |
|  | x |  | x | x | x | x |
|  | x |  | x | x | x | x |
|  | x |  | x |  | x | x |
|  | x |  | x |  |  | x |
|  | x |  | x |  | x | x |
| x |  |  | x | x | x | x |
| x |  |  | x | x | x | x |
| x |  |  | x |  | x | x |
|  | x |  | x | x | x | x |
|  | x |  | x |  |  | x |
|  | x |  |  |  |  |  |
|  | x |  | x |  |  | x |
|  | x |  |  |  |  |  |
|  | x |  | x |  | x | x |
| x |  |  | x | x | x | x |
| x |  |  |  |  | x | x |

## Table 13.   (continued)

| 38 Nonfood Companies by Product Types | Existing Products | |
|---|---|---|
| | Now Adopt Locally | Phase 1 Global |
| 26.   Proprietary drugs, toiletries | x | |
| 27.   Household products | x | |
| 28.   Hair care, small appliances | x | |
| 29.   Writing instruments, lighters | x | |
| 30.   Sanitary protection, health kits | x | |
| 31.   Household products, batteries, food | x | |
| 32.   Proprietaries, pharmaceuticals, cosmetics, perfume | x | |
| 33.   Toys, games | x | |
| 34.   Household products, auto supplies | x | |
| 35.   Proprietaries, pharmaceuticals, razors/blades, candy | x | |
| 36.   Proprietaries, pharmaceuticals | | |
| 37.   Cosmetics, face care | | |
| 38.   No answer | | |
| **34 Food Companies by Product Types** | | |
| 1.   Beverages, food products | | x |
| 2.   Breakfast foods, frozen foods, beverages | | x |
| 3.   Confections, chewing gum | | x |
| 4.   Fast foods | | x |
| 5.   Beer, beverages | x | |
| 6.   Cheeses, condiments, dressings | x | |
| 7.   Potato products | x | |
| 8.   Milk products, cheeses, instant drinks | x | |
| 9.   Ice cream, pasta, canned fruit, chocolate | x | |
| 10.   Fruit drinks, coffee, orange juice | x | |
| 11.   Dry cooking mixes, flour, frozen ref. foods | x | |

| | New Products | | Positive Attitudes on Global New Product Development | | | |
|---|---|---|---|---|---|---|
| U.S. Development Only | Home Country Development | Phase 2 Global New Products | Positive | Essential for Future | Feasible and Practical | More Companies Will Do |
| | x | | x | x | x | x |
| | x | | | | | |
| x | | | x | | x | x |
| | x | | x | x | x | x |
| | x | | | | | x |
| | x | | | | | x |
| | x | | | | | x |
| | x | | | | | |
| x | | | | | | |
| | x | | | | | |
| | x | | | | | |
| | x | | x | | x | x |
| x | | | | | | |
| x | | | | | | |
| x | | | x | | x | x |
| | | | x | x | x | x |
| | x | | | x | x | x |
| | x | | x | | x | x |
| x | | | x | x | x | x |
| | x | | x | | x | x |
| | x | | | | x | x |

# Table 13.   (continued)

| 34 Food Companies by Product Types | Existing Products | |
|---|---|---|
| | Now Adopt Locally | Phase 1 Global |
| 12. Dog/cat foods | x | |
| 13. Diet foods | x | |
| 14. Margarines, cooking oils | x | |
| 15. Confections, candy bars | x | |
| 16. Meat products, snacks, broad ranges of canned/ frozen foods | x | |
| 17. Coffee, breakfast foods, puddings, toppings, juices | x | |
| 18. Breakfast foods, pet foods | x | |
| 19. Frozen foods, soups, sauces, bakery, juices | x | |
| 20. Dry cooking mixes, flour, frosting mixes, snacks | x | |
| 21. Baby foods | x | |
| 22. Fast foods | x | |
| 23. Margarines, cooking oils, dressings, cheeses | x | |
| 24. Fast foods | x | |
| 25. Beverages, snack foods, wines/spirits | x | |
| 26. Breakfast foods, dry mixes, snacks, pet foods | x | |
| 27. Tuna fish products | x | |
| 28. Fruit products | x | |
| 29. Mayonnaise, margarines, cooking oils, corn syrups | x | |
| 30. Bakery goods | x | |
| 31. Chocolate products | x | |
| 32. Tomato products, cooking oils, popcorn | x | |
| 33. Condiments, canned/bottled foods | x | |
| 34. No answer | | |

| New Products | | | Positive Attitudes on Global New Product Development | | | |
|---|---|---|---|---|---|---|
| U.S. Development Only | Home Country Development | Phase 2 Global New Products | Positive | Essential for Future | Feasible and Practical | More Companies Will Do |
| | X | | | | X | X |
| | X | | | | X | |
| | X | | | | | X |
| | X | | X | | | X |
| | X | | X | X | X | X |
| | X | | | | | X |
| | X | | | | | |
| | X | | | | | X |
| | X | | | | | |
| | X | | | | | X |
| | X | | | | | |
| | X | | | | | |
| X | | | | | | X |
| | X | | | | | |
| | X | | | | | |
| | X | | | | | |
| | X | | | | | |
| | X | | | | | |
| X | | | | | | |
| X | | | | | | |
| X | | | | | | |
| X | | | | | | |

Table 14.    Key Executive Attitudes about
Global New Product Development

|  | Nonfood | Food | Total |
|---|---|---|---|
| A. Had a positive attitude about the concept | 25 | 8 | 33 |
| Completely positive | 11 | 2 | 13 |
| Positive but with reservations about implementation | 14 | 6 | 20 |
| B. Had a neutral or indifferent attitude about the concept | 1 | 1 | 2 |
| C. Had a definitely negative attitude about the concept | 10 | 23 | 33 |
| D. No answer | 2 | 2 | 4 |
| Total Companies | 38 | 34 | 72 |

For the future it seems necessary to think in global terms. The world is getting smaller and smaller. *Nonfood*

The type of products sold by our company are all used worldwide. There is no reason not to do it for efficiency reasons. *Nonfood*

If possible, new products should be developed as global brands from the beginning. The ultimate potential long term is greater with the synergy and efficiencies of universal marketing, R&D, operations and logistics. *Food*

Competitors are no longer national but international. A global perspective is required if one wants to survive as a market leader. *Nonfood*

Unabashedly yes. And there's also a need for identical approaches to opportunities in individual markets and/or continents. History and experience has shown us this is very necessary. *Nonfood*

This is a good idea to the extent it is applicable. New product development economics are such that consideration must be given up front to the broadest possible geographic exploration. *Nonfood*

I agree to the extent possible that new products should strive toward a global applicability and appeal. Consumers are becoming more and more similar. In the long run, global marketing should be more efficient and effective. *Nonfood*

Yes, I believe that more and more this will be reality. The costs of new product development and international communications are the driving forces. *Nonfood*

*Positive attitudes but with reservations.*    Another group of executives had a positive attitude about new product development but had reservations about implementation. Their major reservations were:

1. Recognition that product adjustments have to be made—particularly with food.
2. Recognition that the distribution of some product categories might be a problem—example frozen foods.
3. Recognition that in the drug business, local health regulations may require adjustments in dosages, brand names and claims.
4. Recognition that manpower and the organization's ability to carry out global marketing is a complex challenge.
5. Recognition that some product categories are easier to globalize than others.

## Typical comments that were positive but with reservations:

I think it's an excellent strategy. The major caution is to recognize that there are differences in market development and consumer tastes. The global concept will lead us to what would appear to be a considerably more cost effective kind of marketing. *Food*

Yes, I believe that the product and positioning should have global potential, but the specifics (brand name, package graphics) may not be appropriate everywhere. The specific execution of beauty products must be consistent with local fashion trends, looks, etc. I do believe that the product positioning and product itself, however, are totally transportable and should be looked at on a global basis. *Nonfood*

Yes, but not necessarily as "brands." We develop worldwide strategies by category—then fit brands where applicable. Different regulations for over-the-counter drugs exist by country and adjustments have to be made. Also brand names vary by product by country. *Nonfood*

We should strive to achieve this but can't always do so. We want globalization for efficiency but local differences often require changes. *Nonfood*

Yes, generally speaking it would seem to make sense. With our products, however, it is not always practical. But it makes sense because of R&D and development costs. *Nonfood*

It's a great idea in theory. But it may be more difficult to achieve in certain product categories such as food where strong regional businesses exist. Further a company's distribution system may not exist worldwide. For example, a strong frozen food marketer in the U.S. may not possess the capability worldwide and to do so becomes a major capital decision. *Food*

While it simply isn't practical for us to introduce in two or more countries at the same time, brands should be conceived as global brands. It should be recognized, however, they will not be marketable in all countries due to consumer/marketplace differences. Test marketing expansion should follow in as many countries as the organization can handle well as fast as possible. *Nonfood*

Yes, but I don't think it's realistic for our company to do truly global development. We do, however, attempt to develop with multiple country applications in mind. Initial development of global brands will require a management structure and degree of control far beyond our current corporate capabilities. *Nonfood*

Yes, products good for the U.S. or for Europe or then all the developed countries are equally sought. Remember the European Economic Community is now almost as big a market as the U.S. in some categories. But truly global products are rare without some local modification. *Nonfood*

If possible, the concept of global brands should be used. But not to the exclusion of regional opportunities. The global concept gives you the option of dealing with a larger opportunity. *Nonfood*

Yes, for us but it really depends on the product. Some products are easier to position for global use than others. *Nonfood*

We are working toward a global strategy on new products. It's only practical if customer requirements/indications are the same worldwide and the product can be registered/sold worldwide. There are examples were globalization is not practical. (1) Highly localized market with special health problems; (2) ingredients not acceptable locally; (3) lack of acceptance of dosage form such as a suppository. *Nonfood*

Yes, but it really depends so much on the company and the product category. For IBM, it's yes. For ketchup maybe it's no. Only certain mores can be changed unless you create a trend or have a megabudget. *Food*

It does depend a lot on the category. For example, prescription products should be as global as possible. *Nonfood*

The concept is sound. But with regulatory problems which differ from country to country, the implementation is/will be slow for the immediate future. *Nonfood*

I believe it is possible to have a brand that has the same product characteristics worldwide. However, product positioning may have to vary depending on consumer needs and competition, etc. *Food*

*Negative attitudes about the concept.*    Executives who were negative to the idea of global new product development seemed to feel quite strongly regarding the issue. With them it was obviously a controversial point. Their major arguments against the concept were:

1. It was impossible to be universal for their product—particularly if it were a food product. There were too many cultural differences. Consumer needs were not universal.
2. There were vast differences in market development and competition country by country.
3. It was much too complex, slow and cumbersome to implement.
4. It was far better to optimize market by market. The global concept was seen as too restrictive and inflexible. A real straitjacket.

Typical highly negative comments:

For all but a handful of product types, the idea is *nonsense*. Markets are too diverse to make singular positionings, packaging and formulation effective. *Food*

As long as the "image of equity" inherent in the brand is not denigrated, we believe it makes more sense to optimize by major market. Each area of the world has a different set of customers, mores, beliefs, etc. The marketer must design and offer products which address the customer's specific needs/wants which exist in the context of their belief system. *Conglomerate*

I don't believe it should be done. Globalization of brands (products) limits the optimization of that product's potential. Locked in criteria to fit the world limits flexibility. *Fastfood*

Depending on the product, this is generally not a good idea due to regulatory and/or cultural differences in various countries. Using a single brand name on a global basis is very difficult. I've had practical experience in dealing with new products on a global basis. In addition, trademark restrictions in global markets and maintenance fees for these markets are extremely expensive. *Nonfood*

It's not a good idea. The consumer needs and competitive situations are so different country by country that the global approach is doomed to failure. *Food*

It's not practical for our products. Too much variability in local preferences for food and local sources of raw materials. *Food*

It's really too broad. It would slow down new product development if we did testing to ensure global acceptance before introducing a new product. *Nonfood*

I think such a straitjacket would be unwise. It unduly restricts both the U.S. and foreign nation managers from meeting local needs. *Food*

It's a bad idea. There are too many differences in local raw materials to have products absolutely identical. Local tastes also differ substantially. Food tastes differ greatly from country to country. *Fastfood*

With few exceptions, globalization at the conceptual and development stage contributes to inordinate complexity. It is easier to adopt a product to international eccentricities once established as a viable opportunity in the largest market. *Food*

I believe this is very difficult to do. The requirements in each market are too unique. *Food and beverage*

This concept is not very relevant to our business. Market penetration and maturity varies greatly by country. *Food*

I don't think it's a good idea. Conditions, local customs and especially competitive situations differ in each country. *Nonfood*

It is not appropriate at this stage of the brand's development. The arena in which we compete is fragmented, at different stages of development in different countries and has very different competitive sets. *Food*

This would be a fine concept if the benefits consumers were seeking were universal. It's not so in foods. We generally develop new products for each home country. Some of them might be expanded later to other countries. *Food*

*Attitudes about specific aspects of global new product marketing.* Company executives were also asked for their opinions and attitudes about several aspects of global new product development:

1. Did they feel it was a concept which was essential for a company's future success in world sales?
2. Did they feel the concept was practical and feasible?
3. Did they feel it is a concept more and more U.S. companies will pursue?

Table 15.  Executive Attitudes toward Specific Aspects of the
Global New Product Concept

|  |  | Nonfood | Food | Total |
|---|---|---|---|---|
| 1. | Importance to a company's future |  |  |  |
|  | --Essential for success | 17 | 4 | 21 |
|  | --Not essential for success | 18 | 28 | 46 |
|  | --No answer | 3 | 2 | 5 |
|  | Total Executives | 38 | 34 | 72 |
| 2. | Practical and feasible to accomplish |  |  |  |
|  | --Is practical and feasible | 24 | 11 | 35 |
|  | --Is not practical and feasible | 13 | 20 | 33 |
|  | --No answer | 1 | 3 | 4 |
|  | Total Executives | 38 | 34 | 72 |
| 3. | A concept more and more companies will adopt |  |  |  |
|  | --Yes:  More companies will adopt | 30 | 16 | 46 |
|  | --No:  Companies will not adopt | 6 | 11 | 17 |
|  | --Don't know | 1 | 4 | 5 |
|  | --No answer | 1 | 3 | 4 |
|  | Total Executives | 38 | 34 | 72 |

About two-thirds of the executives (46 of 72) believed that global new product development was a concept more and more companies would pursue. Among nonfood executives this was almost 80 percent. Among food executives it was about half (see table 15).

There was much less conviction that global new product development was essential for a company's future or was practical and feasible. Only 29 percent of the executives believed it was essential to the company's future. Among nonfood executives, this was 45 percent; with food executives it was only 12 percent.

About half of all executives thought it was practical and feasible. Again, this was much higher among nonfood executives where about two-thirds agreed. Only 32 percent of the food people felt the concept was practical and feasible.

# 7

# The Critical Issue of Implementation

## Organizing for Global Focus

Some of the executives in our research put it this way: "It may be a great theory—but just try to implement it." Looking ahead, perhaps one of the most important issues in global new product development is how to implement successfully. It's a critical question of organization, structure, and people.

For example, consider organization and structure. The question is: Does the organizational structure allow and encourage people to think globally? A strictly domestic division whose performance is measured by domestic sales and growth is very unlikely to show great concern for the globalization of existing or new products. As one food executive expressed it, "I don't believe the development of global new products would be practical or feasible in a *decentralized* organization where decisions are made at the division or affiliate level."

The problem of global focus in a decentralized organization was dramatically emphasized in a letter regarding this study. It was sent by a top executive of one of the country's most entrepreneurial consumer/industrial goods companies:

> We would like to be of help with regard to your interesting project. Our company, however, is very highly decentralized with more than 40 operating divisions. Each division general manager is responsible for research, development, manufacturing, marketing, and sales in his area of responsibility. And each of these general managers has a great deal of flexibility in structuring the functions which report to him. Thus, it is not possible to give a "company answer" to the majority of items in your questionnaire.

This fact must be dealt with: global new product development is a much more complex process than home-country marketing. As one executive admitted, "Initial development of global brands will require a management structure and degree of control far beyond our current corporate capabilities." Michael Porter of Harvard Business School pointed out that "competing globally creates an exceedingly difficult organizational challenge. A firm . . . must achieve the right amount of geographic centralization and world coordination of activities at the same time it maintains responsiveness to local needs." He went on to explain that the structure must handle a vast amount of "information transfer" in order to coordinate "while at the same time motivating managers in the field to perform."[1] In his latest book, *Competition in Global Industries*, Porter, with the help of Christopher Bartlett, expands even further on this critical coordination problem.[2]

Allen Rosenshine, at the time he was chief executive officer (CEO) of BBDO—one of the world's largest advertising agencies—stated that he believed centralized control was the real problem in implementing a global strategy because this kind of control went against human nature. Rosenshine compared the idea to communism which was attractive "from a philosophic point of view" but difficult "from a human nature point of view." As he put it, "it is a very attractive proposition, it brings out the best in all of us; and yet, it is so contrary to human nature to sacrifice one's own self-interest for the benefit of the whole. . . . Global marketing is a totalitarian system, in a sense . . . it requires coverage and control; it requires centralized authority to basically see to it that people everywhere adhere to what is necessary." So, Rosenshine concludes, "the biggest drawback to the concept has thus far been the basic, human, not-invented-here syndrome."[3]

The human element has indeed proved to be one of the major stumbling blocks in implementing global marketing. As Porter put it, "the human element typically causes the most difficulty."[4] Perhaps an even greater difficulty is the fact that in U.S. new product development programs today, there are very few managers who have an international experience or knowledge. Even if they were convinced the program should be global, very few of them have the background to function on this strategy.

The task of a global new product developer requires a very special talent. As Professor Takeuchi of Hitoshibashi University explained, "the global manager has to be schizophrenic, able to think internationally and be locally responsive simultaneously."[5] There are very few of these managers around. The plain fact is that to effectively implement global new product development will require a whole new breed of global managers. It isn't surprising for *Business Week* to have reported that the "global manager was a hot item." The editorial went on to explain that "as scores of U.S. companies expand overseas or find foreign competitors invading their home turf, they are encountering a critical need for global managers who understand foreign management approaches and cultures. To meet this demand, companies are overhauling and expanding their training programs and are prodding business schools to do the same."[6]

## What the Research Showed about Implementation

The present study showed that for the companies now embarked on phase 2 (globalization of new products), no consistent organizational form was used.

Table 16.   New Product Organization in 8 Companies
Practicing Global New Product Development

| | Phase 2 Companies | | | | | | | |
|---|---|---|---|---|---|---|---|---|
| | A | B | C | D | E | F | G | H |
| **1. New product function:** | | | | | | | | |
| --Corporate | | | (a) | | | | | |
| --Divisional | x | x | x | x | | | | |
| --Both | | | | | x | x | x | x |
| **2. Organizational forms used:** | | | | | | | | |
| --Separate corporate department | | | (a) | | x | | x | (b) |
| --Separate divisional department | x | | x | x | | | x | x |
| --Divisional with going brands | x | x | x | | x | | | |
| --Venture groups | x | | x | x | | | | |
| --New products committee | | | | x | | x | | |
| --New products task force | | | | x | | | | |
| --Home country development for each country | x | | x | | | | | x |
| **3. Top corporate management involved on a regular basis** | x | x | x | x | x | x | x | x |
| **4. Top divisional management involved on a regular basis** | x | x | x | x | x | x | x | x |
| **5. International marketing involved on a regular basis** | x | x | x | x | x | x | x | x |

1.  Corporate new business group focuses on acquisitions in new areas.
2.  Has a worldwide business development group.

The divisional level was the most frequent location of new product responsibility although top corporate management was in all cases "deeply involved in new product development on a regular basis." About half of these companies also had some form of corporate new product department in addition to the divisional department. One company had a worldwide business development group at the corporate level to help keep a global focus (see table 16).

The variation in organizational forms used by "global new product" companies might be expected at this point for several reasons. First, the concept is new and emerging. Some of these companies are not totally "global" in their new product approach at this time. As one CEO put it, "We do both global new product development and new products for home markets. The function is not exclusively one or the other at this point."

Second, as previously mentioned, global marketing is complex. It will take some time for companies to work out the best structure to handle the process.

Third, in the case of conglomerates, there is another practical issue. Some divisions lend themselves more to globalization than others. There is, therefore, a variation by division in the handling of new products.

Fourth, during the transition period to "global" thinking, it is normal, too, that the new product function will continue to vary by corporate culture. One company has for some time found success with a new products committee. Others may have found venture groups effective. Some have kept new products in a separate department; others have traditionally put new products and going brands in the same marketing group.

Clearly at this point, the "global new product" concept has manifested itself in these companies as a critical strategy and thought process. It has not resulted in any typical organizational structure to carry out the process. The most important requirements seem to be that: 1) top corporate management set the "global" strategy and be deeply involved in new product development on a regular basis; and 2) international marketing personnel be involved on a regular basis.

Looking at the total 72 companies in the study, the groundwork appears to be present for the centralized thinking and guidance required in global new product development. This is probably due to the fact that any type of successful new product development—global or otherwise—tends to be more effective if it has top corporate involvement on a regular basis.

More than half of the total sample (39 of 72 companies) had a corporate group involved in the new product function as organized in the company. In addition, about half of the companies stated that top corporate management was deeply involved in new product development on a regular basis (see table 17).

**Some Cautions on Going Global**

The whole issue of organizing for global strategy is hardly new. For many years companies have been discussing the problem of how to best organize for an international operation. As Christopher A. Bartlett put it in his article "MNCs: Get Off the Reorganization Merry-Go-Round," "international companies have been searching frantically for the best way to organize what they can best describe as chaos. There's been no shortage of suggestions from consultants and academic observers but few have worked out. With each new problem that arises, companies have jumped from one idea to the next, sometimes proclaiming reorganizational panaceas one week and renouncing them the next."

Table 17. Organization of the New Product Function
in the 72 Companies Responding

|  |  | Total Companies |
|---|---|---|
| Corporate function involved |  | 39 |
| --Corporate function only: | 5 |  |
| --Corporate and divisional: | 34 |  |
| Divisional function only |  | 33 |
|  | Total | 72 |
| Deeply involved on a regular basis |  |  |
| --Top corporate management |  | 37 |
| --Top divisional management |  | 64 |

With new product work, in particular, the balance of local and global input becomes critical. Bartlett points out that "with one set of pressures suggesting global integration and the other demanding local responsiveness, it is easy to see why executives of many companies thought in either-or terms and argued whether to centralize or decentralize control." Bartlett went on to explain that the managers he talked with had remained very sensitive to the conflicting demands of the situation and had resisted a simple either-or answer. "These managers," he explained, "understood that such a clear-cut answer would not work since both forces are present to some degree in all businesses. Moreover, thinking of strategy in global or local terms ignored the complexity, diversity and changeability of the demands facing them."[7]

In 1977 William Davidson and Richard Harrigan pointed out there were three stages in the evolution of the international marketing function related to new products which became more complex with each stage. The "early stage," when an export manager handled a few existing products as new products overseas, was relatively simple. The "intermediate stage," with the evolution of an international division, often moved from a centralized setup to a more complex, decentralized setup as the overseas operation grew in strength. But the third "advanced stage" involved a "complex multi-product, multi-country stage where organizational problems can become more acute."

Although Davidson and Harrigan had no pat answer for the best organizational structure, they did demonstrate that once top management set the strategy, the effective use of international personnel made a marked difference in the speed with which innovations were introduced overseas. For example, in functionally organized firms where there was an international department, 40 percent of the new products went overseas in two years or less—contrasted to only 6 percent where there was no international department. Results in firms with product line organizations were similar. Here, with companies having an international department, 33 percent of all new products went overseas in two years or less contrasted to 18 percent for companies with no international department. Their study also showed that in globally organized companies, 80 percent of all new products were introduced overseas in two years or less.[8]

One of the best studies on global organization has been researched by William Davidson and Philippe Haspeslagh in 1982.[9] Their findings cautioned against a global product structure as the best way to organize. Before accepting such a structure, they urged companies to ask these key questions:

1. Are foreign operations equally important to each individual business? (Managers who do not depend on foreign operations for a large part of net income are not likely to generate global strategies.)

2. Can the company staff the worldwide business unit manager positions with people who are cosmopolitan in outlook and administrative background? (Previous international exposure among business unit managers is a key ingredient in generating global strategies. Unfortunately, the pool of such people in most U.S. companies is very small.)

3. Does the corporate climate permit risk taking? (Corporate attitudes toward risk have a big influence on the way in which business unit managers treat their more uncertain foreign ventures.)

4. Can the company reduce the loss of foreign experience resulting from the transition to a global product structure? (Many companies have lost experienced international executives and left each worldwide business to learn from its own mistakes.)

5. Is there someone in the company who will continue to strongly promote foreign expansion? (Typically, such advocacy disappears with the international division.)[10]

Davidson and Haspeslagh explain that some companies find a matrix type organization works best for this situation: "effective transfer requires a push from domestic managers and a pull from host country management—two forces the matrix structure uniquely combines." They also point out that for some companies a "rejuvenated international division" can be effective in managing a more complex global strategy.[11]

The global new product activity should, it is believed, be approached with even more caution. Here you are dealing with the company's more innovative people (hopefully) and those who may be even more difficult to handle in the face of lost autonomy or pressure to think globally.

The best advice seems to be to avoid sweeping organizational changes to "go global on new products." Move cautiously with the corporate culture and the talent already in place. Start at the top and be certain top management is dedicated to a global new product strategy. Let it be known that managers will be rewarded for global thinking. Work for that fine balance of local input and global input. Recognize that people retraining will probably be necessary. Start out with a few global projects using, for example, an international new products task force made up from existing managers, if possible. Let the organization evolve and develop. Remember, this is just the beginning of a long-term strategic plan to act and think globally.

## More Effective International Research

It is hardly possible to talk about the implementation of a global strategy without recognizing international research as a critical part of the new equation.

Morten M. Lenrow, the director of marketing research at PepsiCo International, points out that today many multinational companies are thinking in broader terms about research. With the new focus on the similarities between countries, research departments are forced to approach research projects differently. As Lenrow puts it, "the marketing researcher must also seek the commonalities needed to use the world brand concept. It is more important than ever . . . to provide reliable marketing intelligence . . . World brand research requires far more attention to tiny details than would be required in the U.S."[12]

The proper implementation of global new product development will depend heavily on more effective international research. Today British agencies and research firms appear to have the lead in dealing with the complexities of this area. Eileen Cole of Research International believes that few American research companies can offer the same capabilities in international research as some of the British firms. She explains that "British [research] agencies, operating either from their U.S. offices or from the U.K., have become the major suppliers of American corporations' international research needs. . . . British agencies have specialized in the international research field for a long time and are experienced in this highly technical and complex area."[13]

I don't believe it is necessary to expand on all the complexities involved in doing research on a world basis. The important issue is to recognize the need for more effective international research and the change in emphasis that will be required. As Morten Lenrow stated: "The major difference is in the attitude of the people analyzing the data; the emphasis is on finding similarities or common threads to permit the effective use of a global strategy."[14]

# 8

# Global New Product Development: Summary and Conclusions

## Acceptance of Globalization on Existing Products

My first assumption had been that the globalization of markets concept was being utilized by an increasing number of U.S.-based multinational consumers goods companies on *existing* products.

The analysis of current new product programs plus the research study among 137 leading U.S.-based multinational consumer goods companies showed that this assumption was only partially true.

Nonfood consumer goods companies had widely accepted globalization for existing products. About 61 percent (23 of 38) were now involved with existing brand globalization.

However, acceptance was considerably lower with food companies and attitudes toward the concept were much less positive. Only 12 percent (4 of 34) were involved in the globalization of existing brands. This generally negative response among food companies was due largely to the belief that cultural differences in local food and food tastes were too wide.

The study showed, therefore, that globalization is very dependent on product category. In this case, the hypothesis is true for a broad range of existing nonfood products—proprietaries, toiletries, household products, soaps, cigarettes, cosmetics, etc. However, with the exception of some existing products in the breakfast cereal and fast food categories, the assumption did not appear to be generally true for food companies.

## Acceptance of Globalization on New Products

My second assumption was that globalization was not being adopted by U.S.-based multinational consumer goods companies for *new product expansion*.

The analysis of current new product programs and the research conducted both confirmed that this assumption was correct. The study clearly showed that for U.S.-based multinational consumer goods companies the norm was a new product development program with a national boundary, home-country orientation. In spite of the publicity given to the globalization concept, 80 percent of the companies developed new products for home-country use. Successful products in home markets might later be expanded internationally. While 100 percent of the food companies took this approach, it was a somewhat lower percentage (79 percent) with nonfood companies.

A review of the literature, current executive attitudes, and examples of industry training programs further substantiated the fact that new product development is currently national boundary oriented.

The research also indicated that globalization tends to be a two-step process:

Phase 1: Globalization of existing brands
Phase 2: Globalization of new products

Companies tend to start first with a major existing brand which has already achieved success in one or more markets. Once the company has followed a global strategy for an existing product, it is much more apt to consider globalization of the new product function.

In the nonfood category, 23 companies were in phase 1. Eight of these companies, or 35 percent, had already moved into phase 2. Based on executive attitudes, there is every indication that the use of global new product development as a strategy will increase strongly among nonfood companies.

In the food category, only four companies were in phase 1. None of the food companies were reported to be in phase 2. Considering the attitudes of food executives, it would seem highly unlikely that global new product development would increase as a strategy among food companies.

## Modifications Indicated to Globalize Current New Product Programs

The third assumption I made was that to implement global new product development, U.S.-based multinational consumer goods companies would require *major* changes in their current new product programs—changes in philosophy, methodology, and organization.

The analysis of current new product practices and the research conducted both confirmed this assumption. The study clearly showed that with the national boundary orientation now in place, substantial changes in existing new product programs would be required to follow a global strategy.

### Changes in Philosophy and Strategic Planning

Global new product development would have to be an integral part of the company's long-term strategic plan. Such a program is complex, time consuming, and more costly than single market development. It will require top-level vision and support to survive. Global new product development definitely requires a long-term, strategic commitment.

*Changes in Process and Methodology*

Globalization would require significant changes in every important step of the new product development process.

In the *planning stage,* it would be critical:

1. to assess company assets on a global basis.
2. to establish an international policy on R&D utilization.
3. to study new categories and markets on a global basis using cluster analysis and standardized consumer research for each country.
4. to set a global new product policy that includes a priority plan for entrance into each country along with a definition of which brands will be local, regional, or global.
5. to include at the idea generation and concept testing phase the input of company personnel and consumers from at least the top priority countries.

In the *development stage,* it would be critical:

1. to obtain approval of the final creative strategy from managers having a thorough knowledge of the key world areas on the product's priority list.
2. to develop physical product which, as much as feasible, takes into account the legal requirements and the ingredient/cost availability differences for each country.
3. to develop communication, if possible, that relies on basic, universal motivating appeals.
4. to include in all preliminary product and communication testing a sample from at least the key priority countries.

In the *evaluation and commercialization* stage, it would be critical:

1. to establish a global production and costing plan which integrates the product internationally. Standardization of product forms, sizes, and pricing will be important.
2. to test packaging, product, and advertising with a sample that includes at least key priority countries.
3. to include key countries in any quantitative laboratory pretesting and, if called for, test marketing.

4. to be certain the marketing plan establishes a global rollout plan and timetable for key country introduction.

*Changes in Organization and Structure*

The study showed that among the eight consumer goods companies now involved in global new product development, no *one* organizational structure emerged. It was obvious that global new product marketing was complex and companies were feeling their way along as to the best organizational structure to use. The only common characteristic among these companies seemed to be the consistent deep involvement of top management and the international marketing personnel.

The major changes in the organization for global new product development seem to be due to the larger scope, the number of people who need to be involved, and the greatly increased transfer of information required.

Several changes in structure are particularly critical:

1. The structure must allow for the regular input into the new product process from people worldwide with international knowledge and experience.
2. The structure must find the right balance between *headquarters* and *local* input and control of new product development.
3. The structure must provide an environment which rewards managers for global thinking and advances people for making new product decisions in world terms.

The study revealed that there was considerable concern and confusion about the implementation of global new product development. In fact, proper implementation of global new product development may well be the strategy's greatest deterrent. Finding the right people to carry out this complex assignment and developing the right organization to accomplish the mission may, for many companies, be a major obstacle.

As one president of a leading consumer goods conglomerate put it: "I believe strongly in globalization on existing products, but I don't think it's realistic for us to do truly global new product development." He went on to explain that the initial development of global brands would require a management structure and degree of control far beyond their current capabilities.

Another executive of a large food company said "I don't believe the development of global new products would be practical or feasible in our decentralized organization where decisions are made at the division or affiliate level."

The following fact must be dealt with: *global new product development is a much more time-consuming, expensive, and complex process than the tradi-*

*tional single country new product development process.* The basic question companies face is: What kind of an organization and environment will encourage people to think globally? Certainly a domestic new product group which is judged by home-country successes has little incentive to think globally. On the other hand, assigning the responsibility to one centralized group sets up an almost impossible task to accomplish.

The answer lies in finding a structure with the right balance between a global strategy perspective and responsiveness to local conditions. An effective structure must facilitate the transfer of a vast amount of information and, at the same time, motivate and involve people in all parts of the organization. The organization must be able to accommodate global and local thinking simultaneously.

The human element in this structure is, perhaps, the most difficult to handle. Many people resist the centralized control implied by globalization. International marketing people, in particular, have enjoyed a great degree of autonomy.

Another human problem is the shortage of managers who might have the skill to handle the global new product development. The global new product manager will need to be innovative, creative, a tenacious quarterback, possessing marketing know-how and, yet, have the international knowledge to think in world terms. The plain fact is that U.S. consumer goods companies have very few of this new breed of manager. Retraining of personnel will definitely be a part of any global strategy.

Many executives in the study seemed to doubt whether the complexity of global new product development would be worth the trip. After all, even on a home-country basis, new product development is a costly, risky business subject to a high failure rate. The complication of broadening this function to encompass many countries upfront was to many executives unnecessarily unwieldy and complicated. It was as though under these conditions new product development might become so straitjacketed and so hard to coordinate that high failure rates would only increase.

Because of this complexity and the doubts about the validity of universality, it could be that some companies will continue with home-country development yet with much more open lines of communication to international marketing personnel. These companies may also increase the input and involvement of international marketers in the broad planning and strategy of the new product function. This is reportedly the tact that Procter & Gamble is following. Their "global planning" does not focus on standardized, universal global new product development as much as on better coordination between international and new product development; on better planning which will speed up the introduction of new products in several countries once they have proved a success in home markets.

Another point to remember is that even if a company chooses to adopt global new product development, it is unlikely in the foreseeable future that all work on local or regional brands will cease. In many cases, global thinking will be an additive strategy and not a blanket replacement. It is a strategy that will evolve with time; therefore, it is important to not throw out immediately the entire new product structure as it now exists.

# 9

# Implications for Management and Future Research

There is some indication that more U.S.-based consumer goods companies—particularly in the nonfood category—will and should adopt a global strategy on new products. Obviously, where there is a will, there is a way of implementing it. It can be done. Of necessity, foreign-based competition has instinctively been working in this direction for some time. It is inbred in many European and Japanese international marketers, who in turn find U.S. reluctance to accept the idea rather amusing.

Just what are the implications for managers in U.S.-based multinational companies who are considering a global strategy for new product development? Certainly there are no simplistic rules that will guide in a standard way all companies to the promised land. There are, however, important guidelines that can be followed to move management in the right direction.

1. *Global strategy starts at the top and is a top management commitment.* The long-range company outlook must be one which endorses the need for a global viewpoint in all areas of the operation—not just new product development. This outlook will depend on the company and the business in which it is engaged, the industry and product category involved, foreign competition, and the economics of the situation. It must be determined that a long-term global strategy makes more sense for the company than a single country or multidomestic strategy. Global new product development only works as a part of this kind of world oriented business environment. As the research pointed out, very often a company approaches globalization first with existing brands. Global new product development comes as a second step.

2. *Recognize that a worldwide new products intelligence network is critical.* There is no way to proceed in a vacuum. A process must be found to establish a regular flow of new product information and knowledge from both inside and outside the company—knowledge of your own new product activities as well as your competitors; knowledge that can maximize the use of new product talent and experience within your own worldwide organization; knowledge that can be used to predict trends on a global basis; knowledge that can indicate

changes in your product development direction and where best to focus time and resources; knowledge that can allow you to make a fast defensive move against the inroads of a new competitive innovation. Perhaps, there is no other business area where it is more critical to operate with accurate and constantly updated information worldwide.

3. *Remember that successful coordination is by far the biggest problem in implementing a global new product program.* This is a complex problem in motivation and human relations. For most companies it has involved the development of some type of central coordinating group which serves as a bridge and a catalyst between headquarters and local subsidiaries. This coordination process will take time to evolve and fine-tune itself. It requires a great deal of patience and perseverance on the part of all managers.

4. *If at all possible, build your global new product organization from existing worldwide company talent working within your own corporate culture.* In the past when companies have moved too fast with sweeping changes to "go global," some of their best talent and most experienced managers have been lost along the way due to misunderstanding, fear, and improper indoctrination.

Your company is unique because of the particular skill and knowledge of your people. It is management's job to lead people into the new world of global thinking. Recognize, too, that training of staff will be necessary. Company seminars, international conferences, and consistent written communication with affected parties all play their part in developing an organization that rewards people for global thinking. This is particularly true in the area of new product development for world markets.

Also recognize that in the area of recruitment, the need for people with a world viewpoint will be essential. The supply of these managers is limited and even more so when it comes to new product development. Obviously, if a globally oriented organization is to emerge, the talent for global thinking has to be a prime consideration when new staff is added to the company.

5. *Remember, global new product development is a complex and costly program that takes a substantial period of time to fine-tune.* Ultimate perfection in this area, for most companies, will probably be a matter of years and decades—not days and months.

### Important Implications for Food Executives

The apparent rejection of Theodore Levitt's concept of globalization by U.S. food company executives was one of the most significant findings of the study. Of the food executives surveyed, 88 percent said their companies had not adopted a global strategy on *existing* products; 100 percent said they were not using a global strategy on *new* products.

Food executives were particularly negative in their attitude toward global new product development. Typical comments made by food executives expressing this were:

I don't believe it should be done. Globalization . . . limits the optimization of that product's potential. Locked in criteria to fit the world limits flexibility.

This would be a fine concept if the benefits consumers were seeking were more universal. It's not so in foods. We generally develop new products for each home country.

I think such a straitjacket would be unwise. It unduly restricts both U.S. and foreign national managers from meeting local needs.

Each area of the world has a different set of customers, mores, beliefs, etc. The marketer must design and offer products which address the customer's specific needs/wants that exist in the context of their belief system.

Based on past experiences with food in international marketing, these attitudes might well be expected. For some time now food has been considered an extremely "environmentally sensitive" category. It has been one of the prime examples of sensitivity due to differences in economic, sociocultural, and physical characteristics. The need to adapt the food marketing mix for various cultures has been accepted as being far greater than with other categories.[1]

But the real issue now becomes: Is this attitude about food a carryover of the past? Is, in fact, convergence in culture, lifestyle, communications, and travel changing this traditional environmental sensitivity to food? Could it be that food marketers are making a major mistake when it comes to globalization and the rapid changes taking place?

When Theodore Levitt was told of the study's negative results among food executives, his reaction was, "They are dead wrong!" While acknowledging that some foods differ from country to country, Levitt pointed out that there "are still many tastes that transcend borders. . . . Look at Chinese foods, croissants, pita bread, and spaghetti . . . those segments are all over the world. It can be done, it's just a question of how you do it."[2]

There is evidence, too, that European-based multinational food companies do not agree with their U.S. counterparts. *Advertising Age* reported that European food marketers were going global much more aggressively than U.S. food companies. As the trade paper explained, "With small indigenous markets, they are used to moving across national borders. Swiss-based Nestlé . . . is beginning to move products like low calorie Lean Cuisine frozen foods into world markets. Also U.K.-based Rowntree Mackintosh markets Kit-Kat candy bars around the world. On the beverage side, Heineken, based in the Netherlands, has made its beer the best-selling non-indigenous beer in the world." In this same article Theodore Levitt was reported as saying he thought it was all so understandable because "How much chocolate can Nestlé sell in Switzerland? Boundaries are much smaller and they have to do it."[3]

Five years ago, Pierre Liotard-Vogt, then CEO of Nestlé, expressed the viewpoint that food tastes are only habits and are subject to change. He pointed out, for example, how when he was young and living in England, "if you spoke to an Englishman about eating spaghetti or pizza or anything like that, he would just look at you and think that the stuff was perhaps food for Italians.

Now, on the corner of every road in London, you find pizzerias and spaghetti houses."

He also pointed out that the two countries where Nestlé is selling the most instant coffee—England and Japan—were both non-coffee-drinking countries before the war. He concluded, "I do not believe in preconceptions about national tastes. They are habits and they're not the same. If you bring the public a different food, even if it is unknown initially, when they get used to it, they will enjoy it, too. . . . But to believe that tastes are set and can't be changed is a mistake."[4]

Martin van Mesdag, president of a leading British consulting firm, agreed that food and drink products were among the hardest to globalize, yet was amazed at the number that work out on what he calls a "shot in the dark" basis. For example, he pointed out that in 1985 "Britons ate $90 million worth of steaklets and grillsteaks—food products that, 20 years ago, were practically unheard of in Britain. The concept originated in America and is now meeting an enthusiastic response overseas. In the same year, Britons ate $260 million worth of yogurt—a product idea that came from Europe. Other nonindigenous foods popular in Britain now are low-fat cheeses, breakfast cereals, mineral water, pasta, and cookies." Van Mesdag stressed that the important thing to remember is "they were products that had already established themselves in their respective home markets and were brought to Britain with a 'let's try and see' attitude."[5]

In the soft drink and fast foods categories, there continue to be reports of successful international expansion—sometimes with modest adaptation. Perhaps one of the best examples has been the explosion of Diet Coke worldwide. In most of the world, before Diet Coke, there was a question of whether or not a sizeable diet soft drink market even existed. Coca-Cola, Inc., reported that by late 1984 Diet Coke equaled more than 15 percent of Coke's volume in Canada, Norway, Denmark, and Switzerland and that it outsold Pepsi in Ireland, Australia, South America, and Japan.[6]

Dr. Warren Keegan, a leading authority on international marketing, confirmed that U.S. food companies have tended to operate in either one or two extremes—with a completely ethnocentric strategy calling for exact product extensions to all countries or with a polycentric strategy allowing for complete local adaptation in each country. As Keegan explained, "Little integrated global marketing has been attempted on the part of food companies."[7]

The apparent rejection of globalization by the leading food executives in the study could be a serious problem in terms of U.S. competitiveness worldwide and the future success of U.S.-based multinational food companies. The strong U.S. dollar has further complicated the issue. It has given foreign-based multinational food companies the potential to move more aggressively into U.S. markets with penetration pricing. At the same time, it has encouraged U.S.-based food companies to pull back on international operations due to the squeeze in profits overseas.

As one of the few food executives in the study with a more positive attitude about globalization put it, "U.S. markets are becoming increasingly saturated, segmented, and highly competitive—and less profitable. U.S. food companies need to look beyond current markets to grow and survive in years ahead. Cultural differences are softening. We are becoming a world of people that have many more needs and wants and desires in common."

Unfortunately, this informed director of new product planning for one of the country's very largest food companies did not feel that at this time the company had any global strategy on either *existing* or *new* products.

Let us hope, indeed, that when it comes to global new product development, U.S. food companies, facing increasing worldwide competition, will not be caught "asleep at the switch."

## Future Research Indicated

This study and the discussion of the critical issues suggest several additional areas for research in the global new product arena. Here are a few of the most pertinent projects which might be undertaken.

*A study on the feasibility of globalization in the food category.*     One of the most important findings of our study was the rejection by food companies of globalization on existing and new products. A cross-cultural study of the food category and the practicality of globalization for various food classifications would be extremely helpful for the food industry. This study should include research on the practices now employed by foreign-based multinational food companies in regard to globalization of both existing and new food products.

*A study on global new product development in companies marketing non-consumer goods and services.*     Our study focused on U.S. multinational consumer goods companies. It would be extremely valuable to conduct a similar study among U.S. multinational companies engaged in high tech, industrial, agricultural, and the emerging service industries. Successful globalization of new product development will be even more critical in these industries if we are to maintain U.S. competitiveness worldwide. It would also be valuable to compare the progress made on global new product development among these companies and those in the consumer goods category.

*An in-depth study of the leading practitioners of global new product development.*     Our broad-scale approach to the study of global new product development suggests an additional need—a qualitative, in-depth study of some of the leading global new product development practitioners. The sample for this study should include both consumer, service, and high tech/industrial multinational companies. Both U.S. and foreign based organizations should also be covered.

Typical areas to be probed by the research would be: 1) the critical issues which need to be resolved to achieve successful implementation of global new product development; 2) the structure used before and after instituting the global new product program; 3) the staffing and development of personnel; 4) the process used to incorporate global thinking into the planning, development, and evaluation stages of new product development; and 5) an appraisal of the effectiveness of global new product development in terms of cost efficiency, timing, output, and marketing successes.

*A study to identify the product classifications which can be most effectively globalized.* Our study indicated that globalization is product driven. Some product categories evidently lend themselves to globalization more than others. It would be extremely valuable to have a study clarifying which specific product classifications might be easier to globalize and why.

*A repeat study among consumer goods companies to provide a progress report.* So important is the whole area of global new product development that a monitoring of the progress and evolution of the function in U.S. multinational consumer goods companies would be invaluable. A follow-up study would provide an updated picture of what these companies had done with global new product development and how effective they judged the programs to be.

*Research Projects on Special Problem Areas*

In global new product development, there are certain problem areas which suggest very specific research for better understanding and guidance:

1. A study of outstanding global managers? What qualities do they possess? What experience, knowledge, and ability is critical? The value of headquarters versus local experience? What experience in new products is needed for global new product development?
2. A study of training and development techniques for global managers and, in particular, those in global new product programs?
3. A study on the refinement and more effective use of marketing research in global new product development.
4. A study on the refinement and more effective use of advertising research across cultures—particularly related to new products.
5. A study on clustering countries in new ways which go beyond the traditional demographic methods. This might include the use of data on psychographics, lifestyle, values, and the readiness to accept innovations and new ideas.

# Appendix

# Detailed Results of the
# Global New Product Development Study

This study was completed in 1985 among 137 U.S. multinational consumer goods companies, plus 63 subsidiaries and divisions. A discussion of the objectives, methodology, and sample quality is covered in chapter 6. Following are the detailed question by question results of the study.

**Question 1:** What statement best describes how the new product function is organized in your company?

|  | Companies Responding |
|---|---|
| It's a corporate function | 5 |
| It's a divisional function | 33 |
| It's a combination | 34 |
| Total companies | 72 |

If divisions are involved, are they:

|  |  |
|---|---|
| U.S. domestic | 14 |
| International | -- |
| Both | 53 |
| Total companies | 67 |

**Question 2:** Which organizational forms do you currently use for new product development work? Check all those that apply.

|  | Total Mentions |
|---|---|
| Separate new product department-- corporate | 21 |
| Separate new product department-- divisional | 41 |
| New products combined with established brands in a divisional marketing department | 40 |
| Venture groups | 18 |
| New products committee | 19 |
| New products task force | 25 |
| New product development done in each individual country for that country | 26 |
| Other | 2 |
| Total mentions | 192 |
| Total companies | 72 |

### Total Number of Different Organizational Form
### Used by Each Company

| Forms per Company | Number of Companies |
|---|---|
| One | 20 |
| Two | 11 |
| Three | 18 |
| Four | 17 |
| Five | 5 |
| Six | 1 |
| Total | 72 |

**Question 3:** Which of these groups are deeply involved in new product development on a regular basis?

| | Total Mentions |
|---|---|
| Top corporate management | 37 |
| Top divisional management | 64 |
| R&D | 67 |
| New products director | 58 |
| Product managers | 54 |
| International marketing personnel | 31 |
| Advertising agency | 46 |
| Outside new product service | 23 |
| Total mentions | 380 |
| Total companies | 72 |

**Question 4:** A recent Booz, Allen, and Hamilton study showed that many companies follow this type of seven-step process in new product development:
--New product strategy development
--Idea generation
--Screening and evaluation
--Business analysis
--Development
--Testing
--Commercialization

In general, are these the type of steps your company follows in new product development? __Yes __No.  If no, explain differences:

| | Total Companies |
|---|---|
| Yes | 67 |
| No | 5 |
| Total | 72 |

**Question 5:** During the last 12 months has your company made any important changes in the new product development process? __Yes __No. If yes, describe the changes:

| | Total Companies |
|---|---|
| Yes | 19 |
| No | 53 |
| Total | 72 |

**Question 6:** Now let's discuss the <u>geographic focus</u> of your company's new product program. Which statement would be most true for your company?

Our management would not approve of introducing a new product that didn't appear to have a viable sales potential:

|  | Nonfood | Food | Total |
|---|---|---|---|
| In a major part of the U.S. | 8 | 13 | 21 |
| In the total U.S. | 16 | 13 | 29 |
| Beyond the U.S. | 14 | 7 | 21 |
| No answer | -- | 1 | 1 |
| Total companies | 38 | 34 | 72 |

**Breakdown for the U.S.**

|  | Nonfood | Food | Total |
|---|---|---|---|
| U.S. plus one major area | 5 | 3 | 8 |
| North America | 1 | 1 | 2 |
| North America plus one major area | 1 | 1 | 2 |
| Any major world area | 3 | 2 | 5 |
| Worldwide | 4 | -- | 4 |
| Total | 14 | 7 | 21 |

**Question 7:** Your company is involved in selling products internationally. In terms of new product development, which statement best describes your policy?

|  | Nonfood | Food | Total |
|---|---|---|---|
| New products are developed for the U.S. market and the successful products might later be sold internationally. | 7 | 8 | 15 |
| New products are developed both in the U.S. and by our foreign subsidiaries to be marketed in their own home country. If successful, these products might later be expanded internationally. | 21 | 23 | 44 |
| New products are developed up-front as global so that global considerations are built into the brand from the beginning. New products would usually be tested and introduced in more than one country from the start. The new product would not be introduced unless it appeared to have viable sales potential <u>globally</u>. | 8 | -- | 8 |
| No answer. | 2 | 3 | 5 |
| Total companies | 38 | 34 | 72 |

**Question 8:** In terms of selling an <u>existing</u> brand in a foreign country, which statement best describes your policy regarding product, positioning, and communication?

| | Nonfood | Food | Total |
|---|---|---|---|
| With existing brands we let the locals change any part of the mix necessary to adapt the brand to the local country involved. | 15 | 29 | 44 |
| With existing brands we are working toward a universal global strategy and, as much as possible, we try to keep all parts of the mix essentially the same in each country. | 23 | 4 | 27 |
| No answer. | -- | 1 | 1 |
| Total companies | 38 | 34 | 72 |

**Question 9:** Whether or not your company embraces the concept of <u>globalization and global brands</u>, what is your own opinion of the idea that new products should be developed as global brands from the beginning? Why do you feel that way?

**Summary of Attitudes about Global Concept for New Products**

| | Nonfood | Food | Total |
|---|---|---|---|
| Had a positive attitude about the concept. | 25 | 8 | 33 |
| --Completely positive. | (11) | (2) | (13) |
| --Positive but with reservations about implementation. | (14) | (6) | (20) |
| Had a neutral or indifferent attitude about the concept. | 1 | 1 | 2 |
| Had a definitely negative attitude about the concept. | 10 | 23 | 33 |
| No answer. | 2 | 2 | 4 |
| Total companies | 38 | 34 | 72 |

**Question 10a:** Do you think the development of new products as global brands is essential for a company's future success in world sales? __Yes __No. Why do you feel that way?

|  | Nonfood | Food | Total |
|---|---|---|---|
| Believe that the development of new products as global brands is: |  |  |  |
| essential for a company's future sucess in world markets. | 17 | 4 | 21 |
| not essential for a company's future success in world markets. | 18 | 28 | 46 |
| No answer. | 3 | 2 | 5 |
| Total executives | 38 | 34 | 72 |

**Question 10b:** Do you think the development of new products as global brands is practical and feasible? __Yes __No. Why do you feel that way?

|  | Nonfood | Food | Total |
|---|---|---|---|
| Believe that the development of new products as global brands is: |  |  |  |
| practical and feasible. | 24 | 11 | 35 |
| not practical and feasible. | 13 | 20 | 33 |
| No answer. | 1 | 3 | 4 |
| Total executives | 38 | 34 | 72 |

**Question 10c:** Do you think the development of new products as global brands is a concept more and more U.S. companies will pursue? __Yes __No. Why do you feel that way?

|  | Nonfood | Food | Total |
|---|---|---|---|
| Believe that the development of new products as global brands is: |  |  |  |
| a concept more and more companies will pursue. | 30 | 16 | 46 |

**Question 10c (cont.)**

|  | Nonfood | Food | Total |
|---|---|---|---|
| not a concept more and more companies will pursue. | 6 | 11 | 17 |
| Don't know. | 1 | 4 | 5 |
| No answer. | 1 | 3 | 4 |
| Total executives | 38 | 34 | 72 |

# Notes

## Chapter 1

1. Peter F. Drucker, *Managing in Turbulent Times* (New York: Harper and Row, 1980), p. 59.

2. Louis Harris and Associates, Survey (New York, May 1985).

3. Theodore Levitt, "The Globalization of Markets," *Harvard Business Review* (May–June 1983), pp. 92–102. This article also appeared as a chapter in Levitt's book *The Marketing Imagination* (Cambridge, MA: Harvard Business School Press, 1983).

4. M. Ross and D. Padberg, "Small U.S. Trade in Consumer Goods," *The Journal of Consumer Affairs* (Winter 1982), p. 9.

## Chapter 2

1. Theodore Levitt, "The Globalization of Markets," *Harvard Business Review,* p. 92.

2. Ibid., pp. 92–93, 102.

3. Bruce Scott and George Lodge, *U.S. Competitiveness in the World Economy* (Cambridge, MA: Harvard Business School Press, 1984).

4. Robert Reich and Ira C. Magazinner, *Minding America's Business* (New York: Harcourt Brace Jovanovich, 1982).

5. *New York Times* (January 1, 1987), p. 1.

6. "The Controversy Grows," *Advertising Age,* Special Global Marketing Edition (June 25, 1984), pp. 49–50.

7. "Where Global Marketing's Going—A Roundtable with Theodore Levitt," *Marketing and Media Decisions* (December 1984), p. 36.

8. Ronald Alsop, "Efficacy of Global Ad Projects Is Questioned in Firm's Survey," *Wall Street Journal* (September 13, 1984), p. 31.

9. Mitchell Lynch, "Global Marketing Guru," *Advertising Age* (June 25, 1984), p. 50.

10. "Where Global Marketing's Going," *Marketing and Media Decisions* (December 1984), p. 36.

11. Robert O. Jordon, "Multinational Brand Marketing," Lecture Series, Center for International Business, Pace University (May 9, 1984).

12. Ibid., pp. 9–12.

13. Saatchi and Saatchi Compton Worldwide, *The Opportunity for World Brands* (1984), p. 14.

14. *Global Marketing—From Now to the Twenty-First Century* (New York: Global Media Commission—International Advertising Association, 1984), p. 1.

15. "P&G Moving Fast on World Market Entry," *Advertising Age* (June 25, 1981), p. 50.

16. "Gillette Finds World Brand Image Elusive," *Advertising Age* (June 25, 1984), pp. 50, 72.

17. Saatchi and Saatchi Compton Worldwide, *The Opportunity for World Brands,* p. 14.

18. "You're an Advertiser Who's Decided to Take on the World," McCann Erickson advertisement, *Advertising Age* (June 25, 1984), p. 51.

19. Fred Gardner, "A Quartet of Agencies Tunes to Separate Global Notes," *Marketing and Media Decisions* (December 1984), p. 43.

20. Ibid., p. 49.

21. Rebecca Fannin, "What Agencies Really Think of Global Theory," *Marketing and Media Decisions* (December 1984), p. 76.

22. Judy Brott, "The Heat's on Levitt," *Marketing and Media Decisions* (December 1984), pp. 116–17.

23. Fannin, "What Agencies Really Think of Global Theory," p. 76.

**Chapter 3**

1. George P. Murdock, "The Common Denominators of Culture," *The Science of Man in the World Crisis* (New York: Columbia University Press, 1945), p. 145.

2. Everett M. Rogers, *Diffusion of Innovations* (New York: Free Press, 1962).

3. Ernest Dichter, "The World Customer," *Harvard Business Review* (July–August 1962), pp. 113–22.

4. Ilmar Roostal, "Standardization of Advertising for Western Europe," *Journal of Marketing* (October 1963), pp. 15–20.

5. Erik Elinder, "How International Can European Advertising Be?," *Journal of Marketing* (April 1965), pp. 7–11.

6. A. H. Maslow, "A Theory of Motivation" in *Readings in Managerial Psychology,* ed. Harold J. Leavitt and Louis R. Pondy (Chicago: University of Chicago Press, 1976), pp. 6–24.

7. Millard H. Pryor, "Planning in a Worldwide Business," *Harvard Business Review* (January–February 1965).

8. James A. Lee, "The Cultural Analysis in Overseas Operations," *Harvard Business Review* (March–April 1966), pp. 106–14.

9. Howard V. Perlmutter, "Social Architectural Problems of the Multinational Firm," *Quarterly Journal of AIESEC International* (August 1967), pp. 33–44.

10. Arthur C. Fatt, "The Danger of 'Local' International Advertising," *Journal of Marketing* (January 1967), pp. 60–62.

11. Robert Bartels, "Are Domestic and International Marketing Dissimilar?," *Journal of Marketing* (July 1968), pp. 56–61.

12. James Donnelly, Jr., and John K. Ryans, Jr., "Standardized Global Advertising: A Call as Yet Unanswered," *Journal of Marketing* (April 1969), p. 57.

13. John Ryans, "Is It Too Soon to Put a Tiger in Every Tank?," *Columbia Journal of World Business* (March–April 1969), pp. 69–75.

14. Warren J. Keegan, "Multinational Product Planning: Strategic Alternatives," *Journal of Marketing* (January 1969), p. 58.

15. John Fayerweather, *International Business Management: A Conceptual Framework* (New York: McGraw-Hill, 1968).

16. R. J. Aylmer, "Who Makes Marketing Decisions in the Multinational Firm?," *Journal of Marketing* (October 1970), p. 26.

17. Warren J. Keegan, "Multinational Marketing: The Headquarters Role," *Columbia Journal of World Business* (January–February 1971), pp. 85–89.

18. Prakash Sethi, "Comparative Cluster Analysis for World Markets," *Journal of Marketing Research* (August 1971), p. 348.

19. Warren J. Keegan, "A Conceptual Framework for Multinational Marketing," *Columbia Journal of World Business* (November–December 1972), pp. 67–76.

20. Eugene D. Jaffe, *Grouping: A Strategy for International Marketing* (New York: American Marketing Association, 1974).

21. Stewart Henderson Britt, "Standardizing Advertising for the International Market," *Columbia Journal of World Business* (Winter 1974), pp. 39–45.

22. Robert T. Green, William H. Cunningham, and Isabella C. M. Cunningham, "The Effectiveness of Standardized Global Advertising," *Journal of Advertising* (Summer 1975), pp. 25–30.

23. Ralph Z. Sorenson and Ulrich Wiechmann, "How Multinationals View Marketing Standardization," *Harvard Business Review* (May–June 1975), p. 39.

24. David R. McIntyre, "Multinational Positioning Strategy," *Columbia Journal of World Business* (Fall 1975), pp. 106–10.

25. Robert T. Green and Eric Langeard, "A Cross-National Comparison of Consumer Habits and Innovator Characteristics," *Journal of Marketing* (July 1975), pp. 34–41.

26. Edward T. Hall, *Beyond Culture* (Garden City, NY: Amcor Press/Doubleday, 1976).

27. Warren J. Keegan, "Strategic Marketing: International Diversification versus National Concentration," *Columbia Journal of World Business* (Winter 1977), pp. 119–30.

28. Yoram Wind and Howard Perlmutter, "On the Identification of Frontier Issues in Multinational Marketing," *Columbia Journal of World Business* (Winter 1977), pp. 131–39.

29. James Killough, "Improved Payoffs from Transnational Advertising," *Harvard Business Review* (July–August 1978), pp. 102–10.

30. Dean M. Peebles, John K. Ryans, Jr., and Ivan R. Vernon, "Coordinating International Advertising," *Journal of Marketing* (January 1978), pp. 28–34.

31. Igal Ayal and Jehiel Zif, "Competitive Market Choice Strategies in Multinational Marketing," *Columbia Journal of World Business* (Fall 1978), pp. 72–81.

32. Igal Ayal and Jehiel Zif, "Market Expansion Strategies in Multinational Marketing," *Journal of Marketing* (Spring 1979), pp. 84–94.

33. Paul Michell, "Infrastructures and International Marketing Effectiveness," *Columbia Journal of World Business* (Spring 1979), p. 91.

34. Ulrich Wiechmann and Lewis G. Pringle, "Problems that Plague Multinational Marketers," *Harvard Business Review* (July 1979), p. 118.

35. Michael Colvin, Roger Heeler, and Jim Thorpe, "Developing International Advertising Strategy," *Journal of Marketing* (Fall 1980), p. 72.

36. Michael E. Porter, *Cases in Competitive Strategy: Techniques for Analyzing Industries and Competitors* (New York: Free Press, 1980).

37. Harry L. Davis, Susan P. Douglas, and Calvin J. Silk, "Measure Unreliability: A Hidden Threat to Cross-National Marketing Research," *Journal of Marketing* (Spring 1981), pp. 98–109.

38. Johan Arndt, Hiram Barksdale, J. A. Barnhill et al., "A Cross-National Survey of Consumer Attitudes toward Marketing Practices," *Columbia Journal of World Business* (Summer 1982), p. 71.

39. Warren J. Keegan, *Multinational Marketing Management* (Englewood Cliffs: Prentice Hall, 1984), p. 533.

40. Thomas Hout, Michael E. Porter, and Eileen Rudden, "How Global Companies Win Out," *Harvard Business Review* (September–October 1982), pp. 98–108.

41. Theodore Levitt, "The Globalization of Markets."

42. Ellen Day, Richard J. Fox, and Sandra Huszagh, "Global Marketing: An Empirical Investigation," *Columbia Journal of World Business* (Winter 1985), pp. 31–34.

43. Balaji S. Chakravarthy and Howard Perlmutter, "Strategic Planning for a Global Business," *Columbia Journal of World Business* (Summer 1985), pp. 3–10.

44. Gary Hamel and C. K. Prahalad, "Do You Really Have a Global Strategy?," *Harvard Business Review* (July–August 1985), pp. 139–48.

45. Somkid Jatusripitak and Philip Kotler, "Strategic Global Marketing: Lessons from the Japanese," *Columbia Journal of World Business* (Spring 1985), pp. 47–52.

46. E. J. Hoff and J. A. Quelch, "Customizing Global Marketing," *Harvard Business Review* (May–June 1986), pp. 59–68.

47. Roberto Friedmann, "Psychological Meaning of Products: A Simplification of the Standardization vs. Adaptation Debate," *Columbia Journal of World Business* (Summer 1986), pp. 97–104.

48. Michael E. Porter, ed., *Competition in Global Industries* (Boston, MA: Harvard Business School Press, 1986). Also review by Nancy Jackson in *Harvard Business School Bulletin* (December 1986), pp. 8–9.

**Chapter 4**

1. "Taking a Long, Hard Look at Global Marketing," *Marketing and Media Decisions* (December 1984), p. 35.

2. Hirotaka Takeuchi and Ikujiro Nonaka, "The New Product Development Game," *Harvard Business Review* (February–March 1986), pp. 137–40.

3. *Prescription for New Product Success,* American Association of National Advertisers, 1984.

4. John Wolfe, "Study and Look Abroad for Product Ideas," *Advertising Age* (October 15, 1984), p. 10.

5.  Robert Ronstadt and Robert J. Kramer, "Getting the Most out of Innovation Abroad," *Harvard Business Review* (March–April 1982), pp. 94–99.

6.  Michael E. Porter, ed., *Competition in Global Industries,* p. 56.

7.  Theodore Levitt, "The Globalization of Markets," p. 102.

## Chapter 6

1.  *Directory of American Firms Operating in Foreign Countries* (New York: Uniworld Business Publications, 1984).

2.  "The 125 Largest Multinational Companies," *Forbes* (July 2, 1984), p. 129.

3.  "Top 100 Leading Advertisers," *Advertising Age* (September 14, 1984), p. 1.

## Chapter 7

1.  Nancy Day, "Competition in Global Industries," *Harvard Business School Bulletin* (December 1984), p. 78.

2.  Michael E. Porter, ed., *Competition in Global Industries.*

3.  "Is Global Marketing a Wise or Doable Strategy?," *Marketing and Media Decisions* (January 1985), p. 108.

4.  Day, "Competition in Global Industries," p. 78.

5.  Ibid., p. 79.

6.  "The Global Manager Is a Hot Item," *Business Week* (October 31, 1983), p. 49.

7.  Christopher A. Bartlett, "MNC's Get Off the Reorganization Merry-Go-Round," *Harvard Business Review* (March–April 1983), p. 138.

8.  William Davidson and Richard Harrigan, "Key Decisions in International Marketing: Introducing New Products Abroad," *Columbia Journal of World Business* (Winter 1977), pp. 15–23.

9.  William Davidson and Philippe Haspeslagh, "Shaping a Global Product Organization," *Harvard Business Review* (July–August 1982), pp. 125–32.

10.  Ibid., p. 131.

11.  Ibid.

12.  Morten M. Lenrow, "Mapping New Strategy for World Brands," *Advertising Age* (November 1, 1984), p. 40.

13.  Eileen Cole, "Plotting Structural Changes in Industry," *Advertising Age* (November 1, 1984), p. 36.

14.  Lenrow, "Mapping New Strategy for World Brands," p. 40.

## Chapter 9

1.  Warren J. Keegan, *Multinational Marketing Management* (Englewood Cliffs: Prentice-Hall, 1984), p. 39.

2.  John Wolfe, "Global Menu Not Very Tasty to Food Executives," *Advertising Age* (December 17, 1984), p. 32.

3. Dennis Chase, "European Foods Go Worldwide," *Advertising Age* (December 17, 1984), p. 32.

4. "A Conversation with Nestlé's Pierre Liotard-Vogt," *Advertising Age* (June 30, 1980), p. 31.

5. Martin van Mesdag, "Winging It in Foreign Markets," *Harvard Business Review* (January–February 1987), p. 73.

6. Nancy Giges and Lisa Phillips, "Coke Bubbles over Overseas Prospects," *Advertising Age* (October 29, 1984), p. 2.

7. Warren J. Keegan in a personal discussion, January 28, 1985.

# Bibliography

## Globalization and the Key Issues

### Articles

Abu-Ismail, F. F. "Modeling the Dimensions of Innovation, Adoption, and Diffusion in Foreign Markets." *Management International Review,* vol. 22, no. 3, 1982, pp. 54–65.

Adams-Esquivel, Henry. "Global Marketing Needs Specifics." *Marketing News,* May 10, 1985, p. 2.

"Adapting Export Packaging to Cultural Differences." *Business American,* vol. 2, December 3, 1979, pp. 3–7.

Alsop, Ronald. "Countries' Different Ad Rules Are a Problem for Global Firms." *Wall Street Journal,* September 27, 1984, p. 33.

———. "Efficacy of Global Ad Projects Is Questioned in Firm's Survey." *Wall Street Journal,* September 13, 1984, p. 31.

Alter, Stewart. "Creative Outlook Changing on Global Ads." *Advertising Age,* October 29, 1984, pp. 24–28.

Arndt, Johan; Barksdale, Hiram C.; Barnhill, J. A.; et al. "A Cross-National Survey of Consumer Attitudes toward Marketing Practices, Consumerism and Government Regulations." *Columbia Journal of World Business,* vol. 17, no. 2, Summer 1982, p. 71.

Aylmer, R. J. "Who Makes Marketing Decisions in the Multinational Firm?" *Journal of Marketing,* vol. 34, no. 4, October 1970, pp. 25–30.

Bartels, Robert. "Are Domestic and International Marketing Dissimilar?" *Journal of Marketing,* July 1968, pp. 56–61.

Bartlett, Christopher A. "MNC's Get Off the Reorganization Merry-Go-Round." *Harvard Business Review,* vol. 61, no. 2, March–April 1983, pp. 138–46.

Becker, Helmut. "Is There a Cosmopolitan Information Seeker?" *Journal of International Business Studies,* vol. 7, no. 1, Spring 1976, pp. 77–89.

"Benchmark Copy Program." *Colgate Palmolive Advantage,* vol. 1, no. 7, 1983.

Bilkey, Warren J. "An Analysis of Advertisements for Positions in International Business." *Journal of International Business Studies,* vol. 6, no. 2, Fall 1975, pp. 75–78.

Bon, Jerome, and Oliver, Alan. "How a Product's Origin Can Influence Its Image Abroad." *Revue Française du Marketing,* April–May–June 1979, pp. 101–14.

Boote, A. S. "Psychographic Segmentation in Europe." *Journal of Advertising Research,* vol. 22, December 1982–January 1983, pp. 19–25.

Brandt, William K., and Hulbert, James M. "Headquarters Guidance in Marketing Strategy in the Multinational Subsidiary." *Columbia Journal of World Business,* vol. 12, no. 4, Winter 1977, pp. 7–14.

————. "Patterns of Communications in Multinational Corporations: An Empirical Study." *Journal of International Business Studies,* Spring 1976, pp. 57–64.

Britt, Stewart Henderson. "Standardizing Advertising for the International Market." *Columbia Journal of World Business,* vol. 9, no. 4, Winter 1974, pp. 39–45.

Brown, Andrew C. "Europe Braces for Free-Market TV." *Fortune,* February 20, 1984, pp. 74–82.

Buzzell, Robert D. "Can You Standardize Multinational Marketing?" *Harvard Business Review,* November–December 1968, pp. 102–13.

Cain, W. W. "International Planning: Mission Impossible?" *Columbia Journal of World Business.* July–August 1970, p. 53.

Carusgil, S. Tamer. "On the Internationalization Process of Firms." *European Research,* November 8, 1980, pp. 273–81.

Chadraba, P., and O'Keefe, R. "Cross National Product Value Perceptions." *Journal of Business Research,* December 1981, pp. 329–37.

Chakravarthy, Balaji, S., and Perlmutter, Howard. "Strategic Planning for a Global Business." *Columbia Journal of World Business,* Summer 1985, pp. 3–10.

Chase, Dennis. "Global Marketing: The New Wave." *Advertising Age,* June 25, 1984, p. 49.

Colvin, Michael; Heeler, Roger; and Thorpe, Jim. "Developing International Advertising Strategy." *Journal of Marketing,* vol. 44, no. 4, Fall 1980, pp. 73–79.

Cote, Kevin. "Hollywood Glitter May Hurt Global Marketers." *Advertising Age,* September 17, 1984.

Daneke, Gregory A. "The Global Contest over the Control of the Innovation Process: The Case of Biotech." *Columbia Journal of World Business,* Winter 1984, pp. 83–87.

Davidson, William H. "Structure and Performance in International Technology Transfer." *Journal of Management Studies,* vol. 20, no. 4, October 1983, pp. 453–65.

Davidson, William H., and Haspeslagh, Philippe. "Shaping a Global Product Organization." *Harvard Business Review,* vol. 60, no. 4, July–August 1982, pp. 125–32.

Day, Ellen; Fox, Richard J.; and Huszagh, Sandra. "Global Marketing: An Empirical Investigation." *Columbia Journal of World Business,* Winter 1985, pp. 31–34.

Day, Nancy. "Competition in Global Industries: The Promises and Pitfalls of a Global Strategy." *Harvard Business School Bulletin,* vol. 60, no. 6, December 1984, p. 76–87.

Dichter, Ernest. "The World Customer." *Harvard Business Review,* July–August 1962, pp. 113–22.

Dickson, Douglas N. "Case of the Reluctant Multinational." *Harvard Business Review,* vol. 61, no. 1, 1983, pp. 6–18.

"Differences, Confusion Slow Global Marketing Band Wagon." *Marketing News,* January 16, 1987, p. 1.

Donnelly, James H., Jr. "Attitudes toward Culture and Approach to International Advertising." *Journal of Marketing,* July 1970, pp. 60–68.

Donnelly, James H., Jr., and Ryans, John K., Jr. "Standardized Global Advertising: A Call as Yet Unanswered." *Journal of Marketing,* vol. 33, no. 2, April 1969, p. 57.

Doz, Yves L.; Bartlett, C. A.; and Prahalad, C. K. "Global Competitive Pressures and Host Country Demands. Managing Tensions in MNC's." *California Management Review,* vol. 23, Spring 1981, pp. 63–74.

Drazin, Robert, and Howard, Peter. "Strategy Implementation: A Technique for Organizational Design." *Columbia Journal of World Business,* vol. 19, no. 2, Summer 1984, pp. 40–46.

Dugus, Christine. "Global Marketing: Will One Sales Pitch Work Worldwide?" *Ad Forum,* vol. 5, no. 7, July 1984, pp. 20–27.

Dunn, S. Watson. "Effect of National Identity on Multinational Promotional Strategy in Europe." *Journal of Marketing,* vol. 40, no. 4, October 1976, pp. 50–57.

Dymsza, William A. "Global Strategic Planning: A Model and Recent Developments." *Journal of International Business,* Fall 1984, pp. 169–83.

Earle, Richard M. "Global Advertising." *Madison Avenue,* vol. 26, no. 12, December 1984, p. 40.

Elinder, Erik. "How International Can European Advertising Be?" *Journal of Marketing,* April 1965, pp. 7–11.

Fannin, Rebecca. "What Agencies Really Think of Global Theory." *Marketing and Media Decisions,* vol. 19, no. 15, December 1984, p. 74.

Fatt, Arthur C. "The Danger of 'Local' International Advertising." *Journal of Marketing,* January 1967, pp. 60–62.

Fermoselle, R. "International Marketing: You've Got to Know the Territory." *Business America,* vol. 5, September 20, 1982, pp. 16–17.

Flanigan, James. "Multinational, As We Know It, Is Obsolete." *Forbes,* August 26, 1985, pp. 30–33.

Friedmann, Roberto. "Psychological Meaning of Products: A Simplification of the Standardization vs. Adaptation Debate." *Columbia Journal of World Business,* Summer 1986, pp. 97–104.

Gabriel, Peter P. "Adaptation: The Name of the MNC's Game." *Columbia Journal of World Business,* vol. 7, no. 4, Winter 1972, p. 7.

"Global Advertising—Delicate Massage Job." *Forbes,* March 12, 1984, p. 197.

"Global Marketing: Experts Look at Both Sides." *Advertising Age,* April 15, 1985, p. 46.

"Global Marketing: How Marketing Executives Really Feel." *Ad Forum,* vol. 6, no. 4, 1985, pp. 30–31.

"Global Marketing: Strategic Planning from 5 Guidelines." *Marketing News,* vol. 17, no. 22, October 28, 1983.

Green, Robert T.; Cunningham, William H.; and Cunningham, Isabella C. M. "The Effectiveness of Standardized Global Advertising." *Journal of Advertising,* Summer 1975, pp. 25–30.

Green, Robert T., and Langeard, Eric. "A Cross-National Comparison of Consumer Habits and Innovator Characteristics." *Journal of Marketing,* vol. 39, no. 3, July 1975, pp. 34–41.

Halfhill, D. S. "Multinational Marketing Strategy: Implications of Attitudes toward Country of Origin." *Management International Review,* vol. 20, no. 4, 1980, pp. 26–30.

Hall, Edward T., and Hall, Elizabeth. "How Cultures Collide." *Psychology Today,* July 1976, pp. 67–97.

Hamel, Gary, and Prahalad, C. K. "Do You Really Have a Global Strategy?" *Harvard Business Review,* July–August 1985, pp. 139–48.

Harrell, G. D. "Multinational Strategic Market Portfolios." *MSU Business Topics,* vol. 29, Winter 1981, pp. 5–15.

Hill, John S., and Still, Richard R. "Adapting Products to LDC Tastes." *Harvard Business Review,* vol. 62, no. 2, March–April 1984, p. 92.

———. "Effects of Urbanization on Multinational Product Planning: Markets in Lesser-Developed Countries." *Columbia Journal of World Business,* vol. 19, no. 2, Summer 1984, pp. 62–67.

Hoff, E. J., and Quelch, J. A. "Customizing Global Marketing." *Harvard Business Review,* May–June 1986, pp. 59–68.

Hornik, J. "Comparative Evaluation of International vs. National Advertising Strategies." *Columbia Journal of World Business,* vol. 15, Spring 1980, pp. 36–45.

Hout, Thomas; Porter, Michael E.; and Rudden, Eileen. "How Global Companies Win Out." *Harvard Business Review,* vol. 60, no. 5, September–October 1982, pp. 98–108.

Hulbert, J. M.; Brandt, William K.; and Richers, Raimar. "Marketing Planning in the Multinational Subsidiary: Practices and Problems." *Journal of Marketing,* vol. 44, Summer 1980, pp. 7–15.

Jaffe, Eugene D., and Ramut-Gan. "Are Domestic and International Marketing Dissimilar? An Assessment." *Management International Review,* vol. 20, no. 3, June 1980, p. 83.

Jatusripitak, Somkid, and Kotler, Philip. "Strategic Global Marketing: Lessons from the Japanese." *Columbia Journal of World Business,* Spring 1985, pp. 47–52.

Johanson, J., and Vahlne, Jan-Erik. "The Internationalization Process of the Firm." *Journal of International Business Studies,* Spring/Summer 1977, pp. 23–32.

Jordon, R. O. "Targeting International Marketing." *Telecommunications,* vol. 17, April 1983, p. 88.

Kaufman, Lionel. "Are Our Print Media Going Global?" *Marketing and Media Decisions,* vol. 19, no. 15, December 1984, p. 70.

Keefe, V. P. "Language Translation Is the Missing Link in Marketing." *Business American,* vol. 2, September 24, 1979, pp. 6–7.

Keegan, Warren J. "A Conceptual Framework for Multinational Marketing." *Columbia Journal of World Business,* vol. 7, no. 6, November–December 1972, p. 67.

————. "Multinational Marketing Control." *Journal of International Business Studies,* vol. 3, no. 2, Fall 1972, p. 33.

————. "Multinational Marketing: The Headquarters Role." *Columbia Journal of World Business,* January–February 1971, pp. 85–89.

————. "Multinational Product Planning: Strategic Alternatives." *Journal of Marketing,* January 1969, p. 58.

————. "Strategic Marketing: International Diversification versus National Concentration." *Columbia Journal of World Business,* vol. 12, no. 4, Winter 1977, p. 120.

Killough, James. "Improved Payoffs from Transnational Advertising." *Harvard Business Review,* July–August 1978, pp. 102–10.

Kimball, Wendy. "B&D Turning to Global Marketing." *Advertising Age,* October 29, 1984, p. 52.

Klippel, Eugene R., and Boewadt, Robert J. "Attitude Measurement as a Strategy Determinant for Standardization of Multinational Advertising." *Journal of International Business Studies,* vol. 5, Spring 1974, pp. 39–50.

Kuin, Pieter. "The Magic of Multinational Management." *Harvard Business Review,* November–December 1972, pp. 89–97.

Lenrow, Morten M. "Mapping New Strategy for World Brands." *Advertising Age,* November 1, 1984, pp. 40–43.

Levenson, Marc. "The Pitfalls of Global Restrictions." *Dun's Business Month,* October 1986, pp. 40–43.

Levitt, Theodore. "The Globalization of Markets." *Harvard Business Review,* vol. 61, no. 3, May–June 1983, pp. 92–102.

Maisonrouge, Jacques G. "The Mythology of Multinationalism." *Columbia Journal of World Business,* vol. 9, no. 1, Spring 1974, p. 7.

McIntyre, David R. "Multinational Positioning Strategy." *Columbia Journal of World Business,* vol. 10, no. 3, Fall 1975, pp. 106–10.

Michell, Paul. "Infrastructures and International Marketing Effectiveness." *Columbia Journal of World Business,* vol. 14, no. 1, Spring 1979, p. 91.

"Multinationals Tackle Global Marketing." *Advertising Age,* vol. 55, no. 36, June 25, 1984, p. 50.

Narayana, C. L. "Aggregate Images of American and Japanese Products: Implications on International Marketing." *Columbia Journal of World Business,* vol. 16, Summer 1981, pp. 31–35.

Niffenegger, P., and White, J. "How European Retailers View American Imported Products, a Product Image Study." *Academy of Marketing,* Summer 1982, pp. 281–92.

O'Brien, Wally. "Realities of Global Marketing." *Advertising Age,* December 10, 1984, p. 18.

Partanen, Juha. "On National Consumption Profiles—Trend toward International Standardization." *European Research,* January 1979, pp. 27–37.

Paskowski, Marianne. "U.S. Programmers Face Off for Global Challenge." *Marketing and Media Decisions,* vol. 19, no. 15, December 1984, p. 56.

Paskowski, Marianne; Fannin, Rebecca; Gardner, Fred; and Jereski, Laura. "A Quartet of Agencies Tunes to Separate Global Notes." *Marketing and Media Decisions,* vol. 19, no. 15, December 1984, p. 43.

Patterson, Jere. "Coordinating International Advertising." *International Advertiser,* December 1967, pp. 35–38.

Peebles, Dean M.; Ryans, John K.; and Vernon, Ivan R. "Coordinating International Advertising." *Journal of Marketing,* vol. 42, no. 1, January 1978, pp. 28–34.

————. "A New Perspective on Advertising Standardization." *European Journal of Marketing,* 1977, pp. 566–76.

Perlmutter, Howard V., and Heenan, David A. "How Multinational Should Your Managers Be?" *Harvard Business Review,* vol. 52, no. 6, November 1974, p. 121.

————. "Social Architectural Problems of the Multinational Firm." *Quarterly Journal of AIESEC International,* vol. 3, no. 3, August 1967, pp. 33–44.

Prahalad, C. K. "Strategic Choices in Diversified MNC's." *Harvard Business Review,* July–August 1976, pp. 67–78.

Pryor, Millard H. "Planning in a Worldwide Business." *Harvard Business Review,* January–February 1965, pp. 130–39.

Reitman, Judith. "Europe's High Tech Glamour." *Marketing and Media Decisions,* vol. 19, December 1984, p. 62.

Ricks, D. A. "Products that Crashed into the Language Barrier: Naming Products for Foreign Markets." *Business Society Review,* Spring 1983, pp. 46–50.

Rogosky, Wolff D. "On the Sense of International Advertising Campaigns." *Harvard Manager,* April 1, 1979, pp. 74–75.

Roostal, Ilmar. "Standardization of Advertising for Western Europe." *Journal of Marketing,* October 1963, pp. 15–20.

Root, F. R. "Why Every Company Needs a Strategy for Global Competition." *Management International Review,* vol. 71, May 1982, p. 34.

Roth, Robert F. "Who Says 'Locals' Know Best." *Advertising World,* Spring 1979, pp. 32–33.

Rubinger, Bruce. "U.S. Firms Urged to Think Global." *Journal of Commerce,* October 30, 1986, pp. 3A–4A.

Ryans, John K. "Is It Too Soon to Put a Tiger in Every Tank?" *Columbia Journal of World Business,* March–April 1969, pp. 69–75.

Sands, Saul. "Can You Standardize International Marketing Strategy?" *Journal of the Academy of Marketing Science,* vol. 7, Winter–Spring 1979, pp. 117–34.

Saporito, Bill. "Black and Decker's Gamble on Globalization." *Fortune,* vol. 109, no. 10, May 14, 1984, pp. 40–48.

Schiffman, L. G.; Dillon, W. R.; and Ngumah, F. E. "The Influence of Subcultural and Personality Factors on Consumer Acculturation." *Journal of International Business Studies,* vol. 12, no. 2, Fall 1981, pp. 137–44.

Schleifer, Stephen, and Dunn, S. Watson. "Relative Effectiveness of Advertisements of Foreign and Domestic Origin." *Journal of Marketing Research,* August 1968, pp. 296–99.

Schollhammer, Hans. "Long Range Planning in Multinational Firms." *Columbia Journal of World Business,* September–October 1971, pp. 79–86.

Shearer, John C. "The External and Internal Manpower Resources of Multinational Corporations." *Columbia Journal of World Business,* vol. 9, no. 2, Summer 1974, pp. 9–17.

Shuptine, F. K., and Toyne, B. "International Marketing Planning: A Standardized Process." *Journal of International Marketing,* vol. 1, no. 1, 1981, pp. 16–28.

Simmonds, Kenneth. "Multinational? Well, Not Quite." *Columbia Journal of World Business,* Fall 1966, pp. 115–22.

Sirota, David, and Greenwood, J. Michael. "Understand Your Overseas Workforce." *Harvard Business Review,* vol. 49, no. 1, January 1971, p. 53.

Sorenson, Ralph Z., and Wiechmann, Ulrich. "How Multinationals View Marketing Standardization." *Harvard Business Review,* vol. 53, no. 3, May–June 1975, p. 39.

Spencer, William I. "Who Controls MNC's?" *Harvard Business Review,* vol. 53, no. 6, November 1975, p. 97.

"Taking a Long, Hard Look at Global Marketing." *Marketing and Media Decisions,* vol. 19, no. 15, December 1984, p. 34.

Terpstra, Vern. "International Product Policy: The Role of Foreign R&D." *Columbia Journal of World Business,* vol. 12, no. 4, Winter 1977, p. 24.

Terpstra, Vern, and Aydin, N. "Marketing Know-How Transfers by Multinationals." *Journal of International Business Studies,* vol. 12, no. 3, Winter 1981, pp. 35–48.

Thackray, John. "Much Ado about Global Marketing." *Across the Board,* April 1985, pp. 38–46.

Urban, Christine. "A Cross National Comparison of Consumer Media Use Patterns." *Columbia Journal of World Business,* vol. 12, no. 4, Winter 1977, p. 53.

Venkatesh, Alladi, and Wilemon, D. "American and European Product Managers: A Comparison." *Columbia Journal of World Business,* vol. 15, no. 3, Fall 1980, p. 67.

"Waking Up to Global Marketing." *Advertising Age,* December 10, 1984, p. 14.

Walvoord, R. W. "Foreign Market Entry Strategies." *Advertising Management Journal,* Spring 1983, pp. 14–26.

Ward, James J. "Product and Promotion Adaptation by European Firms in the U.S." *Journal of International Business Studies,* vol. 4, no. 1, Spring 1973, pp. 79–86.

Weber, J. A. "Comparing Growth Opportunities in the International Marketplace." *Management International Review,* vol. 19, no. 1, 1979, pp. 47–56.

———. "Worldwide Strategies for Market Segmentation." *Columbia Journal of World Business,* vol. 9, no. 4, Winter 1974, pp. 31–38.

"Where Global Marketing's Going—A Roundtable with Theodore Levitt." *Marketing and Media Decisions,* vol. 19, no. 15, December 1984, p. 36.

Widing, J. William, Jr. "Reorganizing Your Worldwide Business." *Harvard Business Review,* vol. 51, no. 3, May–June 1973, p. 153.

Wiechmann, Ulrich. "Integrating Multinational Marketing Activities." *Columbia Journal of World Business,* vol. 9, no. 4, Winter 1974, pp. 7–16.

———. "Intercultural Communication and the MNC Executive." *Columbia Journal of World Business,* vol. 9, no. 4, Winter 1974, pp. 23–28.

Wiechmann, Ulrich, and Pringle, Lewis G. "Problems that Plague Multinational Marketers." *Harvard Business Review,* vol. 57, no. 4, July–August 1979, p. 118.

Wileman, David, and Venkgtesh, Allad. "American and European Product Managers: A Comparison." *Columbia Journal of World Business,* vol. 15, no. 3, Fall 1980, p. 67.

Wind, Yoram; Douglas, Susan P.; and Perlmutter, Howard V. "Guidelines for Developing International Marketing Strategies." *Journal of Marketing,* vol. 37, no. 2, April 1973, pp. 14–23.

**Books and Reports**

Aharoni, Yair, and Baden, Clifford. *Business in the International Environment.* Boulder, Colo.: Westview Press, 1977.

Baxter, J. C., and Ryans, John K., Jr. *Multinational Marketing: Dimensions in Strategy.* Columbus, Ohio: Grid Publishing, 1975.

Beeth, Gunnar. *International Management Practice: An Insider's View.* New York: AMACOM, 1973.

Cateora, Philip R. *Strategic International Marketing.* Homewood, Ill.: Dow Jones-Irwin, 1985.

Daniels, John D.; Ogram, Ernest W.; and Radebaugh, Lee H. *International Business: Environments and Operations.* Reading, Mass.: Addison-Wesley, 1976.

Davidson, William H. *Global Strategic Management.* New York: John Wiley and Sons, 1982.

Davis, Stanley M. *Managing and Organizing Multinational Corporations.* New York: Pergamon Press, 1979.

Eger, John M. *Global Marketing: From Now to the Twenty-First Century.* New York: International Advertising Association Booklet, Global Media Commission, 1984.

Fayerweather, John. *International Business Management: A Conceptual Framework.* New York: McGraw-Hill. 1968.

————. *International Business Strategy and Administration.* Cambridge, Mass.: Ballinger, 1982.

————. *International Marketing.* Englewood Cliffs, N.J.: Prentice-Hall, 1965.

Griggs, Lewis, and Copeland, Lennie. *Going International: How to Make Friends and Deal Effectively in the Global Marketplace.* New York: Random House, 1985.

Grub, Phillip, and Kaskimies, Mika. *International Marketing in Perspective.* Helsinki: Sininen Kirja Oy, 1971.

Gunnar, Beth. *International Management Practice: An Insider's View.* New York: AMACOM, 1983.

Hall, Edward T. *Beyond Culture.* Garden City: Anchor Press/Doubleday, 1976.

Haner, F. T. *Global Business Strategy for the 1980s.* New York: Praeger, 1980.

Jaffe, Eugene D. *Grouping: A Strategy for International Marketing.* New York: AMACOM, 1974.

Jordon, Robert O. *Multinational Brand Marketing: Guidelines for Success.* New York: Pace Center for International Business Studies, 1984.

Kahler, Ruel, and Kramer, Roland. *International Marketing.* Fourth ed. Cincinnati: South-Western Publishing, 1977.

Liander, Bertil; Terpstra, Vern; Yoshino, M. Y.; and Sherbini, Aziz. *Comparative Analysis for International Marketing.* Newton, Mass.: Allyn and Bacon, 1967.

Majaro, Simon. *International Marketing: A Strategic Approach to World Markets.* Winchester, Mass.: Allen & Unwin, 1982.

Miracle, Gordon, and Albaum, Gerald. *International Marketing Management.* Homewood, Ill.: R. D. Irwin, 1970.

Moschis, George P., and Alexandrides, C. G. *Export Marketing Management.* New York: Praeger, 1977.

Murdock, George P. "The Common Denominator of Culture" in *The Science of Man in the World Crisis.* Ed. by Ralph Linton. New York: Columbia University Press, 1945.

Ohmae, Kenichi. *Triad Power: The Coming Shape of Global Competition.* New York: Free Press, 1985.

Porter, Michael E., ed. *Competition in Global Industries.* Boston: Harvard Business School Press, 1986.

Ricks, David A. *Big Business Blunders: Mistakes in Multinational Marketing.* Homewood, Ill.: Dow Jones-Irwin, 1983.

Robinson, Richard D. *Internationalization of Business: An Introduction.* Chicago: Dryden Press, 1984.

Robock, S.; Simmonds, K.; and Zwick, J. *International Business and Multinational Enterprises.* Homewood, Ill.: R. D. Irwin, 1977.

Rodgers, F. G., and Shook, Robert L. *The IBM Way: Insights into the World's Most Successful Marketing Organization.* New York: Harper & Row, 1986.

Saatchi and Saatchi Compton Worldwide. *The Opportunity for World Brands.* London: 1984.

Steiner, George A., and Cannon, Warren M. *Multinational Corporate Planning.* New York: Macmillan, 1966.

Stopford, John, and Well, Louis T., Jr. *Managing the Multinational Enterprise.* New York: Basic Books, 1972.

Terpstra, Vern. *International Dimensions of Marketing.* Boston, Mass.: Kent Publishing Company, 1982.

————. *International Marketing.* Second ed. Hinsdale, Ill.: Dryden Press, 1978.

Terpstra, Vern, and David, Kenneth. *The Cultural Environment of International Business.* Cincinnati: South-Western Publishing Company, 1985.

Thorelli, Hans, and Becker, Helmut. *International Marketing Strategy.* New York: Pergamon Press, 1980.

Vernon, Raymond, and Well, Louis T., Jr. *Manager in the International Economy.* Englewood Cliffs: Prentice-Hall, 1981.

Walsh, L. S. *International Marketing.* Macdonald and Evans, 1981.

## New Product Development

### Articles

Ayal, Igal. "International Product Life Cycle: A Reassessment and Product Policy Implications." *Journal of Marketing,* vol. 45, no. 4, Fall 1981, pp. 91–96.

Ayal, Igal, and Zif, Jehiel. "Competitive Market Choice Strategies in Multinational Marketing." *Columbia Journal of World Business,* vol. 13, no. 3, Fall 1978, p. 72–81.

————. "Market Expansion Strategies in Multinational Marketing." *Journal of Marketing,* vol. 43, no. 2, Spring 1979, pp. 84–94.

Blattberg, R. C.; Beusing, Thomas; and Sen, Subrata K. "Segmentation Strategies for New National Brands." *Journal of Marketing,* vol. 44, no. 4, Fall 1980, pp. 59–67.

Boote, Alfred S. "Market Segmentation by Personal Values and Salient Product Attributes." *Journal of Advertising Research,* vol. 21, no. 1, February 1981, pp. 29–35.

Calantone, Roger, and Cooper, Robert. "New Product Scenarios: Prospects for Success." *Journal of Marketing,* vol. 45, no. 2, Spring 1981, pp. 48–60.

Carlsson, Christer; Olof-Hansen, Sten. "Innovation and Export Market Strategies in the Pharmaceutical Industry." *Management International Review,* vol. 22, no. 3, 1982, pp. 45–53.

Corbin, R. "A New Structure for Developing New Products." *SAM Advanced Management Journal,* vol. 47, Summer 1982, pp. 4–11.

Cosmas, S. C., and Sheth, J. N. "Identification of Opinion Leaders across Cultures: An Assessment for Use in the Diffusion of Innovations and Ideas." *Journal of International Business Studies,* vol. 11, no. 1, Spring–Summer 1980, pp. 60–73.

Crawford, C. Merle. "Defining the Charter for Product Innovation." *Sloan Management Review,* vol. 22, no. 1, Fall 1980, pp. 3–12.

————. "Marketing Research and the New Product Failure Rate." *Journal of Marketing,* vol. 41, no. 2, April 1977, pp. 51–61.

Currin, I. S. "Using Segmentation Approaches for Better Prediction and Understanding from Consumer Mode Choice Models." *Journal of Marketing Research,* vol. 18, no. 3, August 1981, pp. 301–9.

Davidson, William, and Harrigan, Richard. "Key Decisions in International Marketing: Introducing New Products Abroad." *Columbia Journal of World Marketing,* vol. 12, no. 4, Winter 1977, p. 15.

Day, George S. "Diagnosing the Product Portfolio." *Journal of Marketing,* vol. 41, April 1977, pp. 29–38.

————. "The Product Life Cycle: Analysis and Applications Issues." *Journals of Marketing,* vol. 45, Fall 1981, pp. 60–67.

Dean, Joel. "Pricing Policies for New Products." *Harvard Business Review,* vol. 54, no. 6, November–December 1976, pp. 141–53.

Drucker, Peter F. "The Discipline of Innovation." *Harvard Business Review,* May–June 1985, pp. 67–72.

Giddy, Ian H. "The Demise of the Product Cycle Model in International Business Theory." *Columbia Journal of World Business,* vol. 13, no. 1, Spring 1978, p. 90.

Grayson, Robert A. "The Undetected Causes for New Product Failure." *The Journal of Consumer Marketing,* vol. 1, no. 3, 1984, p. 53.

Green, P. E., and Goldberg, S. M. "A General Approach to Product Design Optimization via Conjoint Analysis." *Journal of Marketing,* vol. 45, no. 3, Summer 1981, pp. 17–37.

Haspeslagh, Philippe. "Portfolio Planning: Uses and Limits." *Harvard Business Review,* January–February 1982, pp. 58–73.

Howard, Niles. "A New Way to View Consumers." *Dun's Review,* vol. 117, no. 8, August 1981, p. 42.

Hulse, Carolyn. "Popular Categories Cross Cultural Boundaries." *Advertising Age,* December 24, 1984, p. 17.

Jackson, B., and Shapiro, Benson. "New Way to Make Product Line Decisions." *Harvard Business Review,* vol. 57, May–June 1979, pp. 139–49.

Jobbers, D. "Test Marketing—An Evaluation of More Recent Micro-Marketing Methods." *Management Decisions,* vol. 17, 1979, pp. 119–41.

Josaitas, Bob. "Explore New Export Markets via Entry Pricing." *American Import-Export Bulletin,* July 1981, p. 54.

Klavans, Richard; Shanley, Mark; and Evan, William M. "The Management of International Corporate Ventures: Entrepreneurship and Innovation." *Columbia Journal of World Business,* Summer 1985, pp. 21–27.

Lawton, Leigh, and Parasuraman, A. "The Impact of the Marketing Concept on New Product Planning." *Journal of Marketing,* vol. 44, no. 1, Winter 1980, pp. 19–25.

Lentini, Cecilla. "Test Marketing: Tomorrow and Tomorrow . . . Whither the Method?" *Advertising Age,* vol. 22, February 1982, p. M9.

Lorsch, Jay W., and Lawrence, Paul R. "Organizing for Product Innovation." *Harvard Business Review,* January–February 1965, pp. 109–22.

Mahajan, Vijay, and Muller, Eitan. "Innovation Diffusion and New Product Growth Models in Marketing." *Journal of Marketing,* vol. 43, no. 4, Fall 1979, pp. 55–68.

Massey, Anne. "Why a New Product Fails." *Marketing,* vol. 6, July 29, 1981, pp. 23–24.

McDonough, Edward F., and Spital, Francis C. "Quick Response New Product Development." *Harvard Business Review,* vol. 62, September–October 1984, p. 52.

Murugasu, P. M. "Selecting Products for Export Development." *International Trade Forum,* vol. 15, October–December 1979, pp. 4–7.

Naraasimhan, C., and Sen, S. K. "New Product Models for Test Market Data." *Journal of Marketing,* vol. 47, Winter 1983, pp. 11–24.

Peters, Michael P. "The Role of Planning in the Marketing of New Products." *Planning Review,* vol. 8, November 1980, pp. 24–27.

Quinn, James Brian. "Managing Innovation: Controlled Chaos." *Harvard Business Review,* May–June 1985, pp. 73–84.

Resnick, Alan J.; Turney, Peter B.; and Mason, J. Barry. "Marketers Turn to 'Countersegmentation.'" *Harvard Business Review,* September–October 1979, pp. 100–106.

Robertson, Thomas. "The Process of Innovation and the Diffusion of Innovation." *Journal of Marketing,* vol. 31, January 1967, pp. 14–19.

Rogers, Everett M. "New Product Adoption and Diffusion." *Journal of Consumer Research,* March 1976, pp. 290–301.

Ronstadt, Robert, and Kramer, Robert J. "Getting the Most Out of Innovation Abroad." *Harvard Business Review,* vol. 60, no. 2, March–April 1982, pp. 94–99.

Rugman, Alan M., and Bennett, Jocelyn. "Technology Transfer and World Product Mandating." *Columbia Journal of World Business,* Winter 1982, pp. 58–62.

Schnee, Jerome E. "International Shifts in Innovative Activity: The Case of Pharmaceuticals." *Columbia Journal of World Business,* vol. 13, no. 1, Spring 1978, p. 112.

Shocker, Allan D., and Srinivasan, V. "Consumer Based Methodology for Identification of New Product Ideas." *Management Science,* vol. 20, no. 6, February 1974, p. 921.

Smallwood, John E. "The Product Life Cycle: A Key to Strategic Marketing Planning." *MSU Business Topics,* vol. 21, Winter 1973, p. 29.

Stein, Phillip W. "The Role of the Product Manager in New Product Development." *Marketing News,* October 1, 1972, p. 4.

Takeuchi, Hirotaka, and Nonaka, Ikujiro. "The New Product Development Game." *Harvard Business Review,* January–February 1986, pp. 137–46.

Tauber, Edward M. "Forecasting Sales Prior to Test Market." *Journal of Marketing,* vol. 41, no. 1, January 1977, pp. 80–84.

————. "New Criteria for Concept Evaluation." *The Journal of Consumer Marketing,* vol. 1, no. 3, 1984, p. 13.

Terpstra, Vern. "On Marketing Appropriate Products in Developing Countries." *Journal of International Marketing,* vol. 1, 1981, pp. 3–15.

Ting, Wenlee. "The Product Development Process in NIC Multinationals." *Columbia Journal of World Business,* vol. 17, no. 1, Spring 1982, pp. 76–81.

von Hippel, Eric. "Get New Products from Customers." *Harvard Business Review,* vol. 60, no. 2, March–April 1982, pp. 117–22.

Weigand, Robert E. "Fit Products and Channels to Your Markets." *Harvard Business Review,* vol. 55, January–February 1977, pp. 95–105.

Weller, D. "Export Product Development: Testing the New Product." *International Trade Forum,* vol. 17, January–March 1981, pp. 16–17.

————. "Export Product Strategies." *International Trade Forum,* vol. 15, July–September 1979, pp. 8–10.

————. "Using Market Research for Product Development (Testing in Different Countries)." *International Trade Forum,* vol. 16, April–June 1980, pp. 16–18.

Wilton, Peter, and Pessemier, Edgar. "Forecasting the Ultimate Acceptance of an Innovation: The Effects of Information." *Journal of Consumer Research,* vol. 8, no. 2, September 1981, p. 162.

Wolfe, John. "Study and Look Abroad for Product Ideas." *Advertising Age,* October 15, 1984, p. 10.

Zufryden, F. S. "Zipmap—A Zero-One Integer Programming Model for Market Segmentation and Product Positioning. *Journal of Operational Research Society,* vol. 30, no. 1, January 1979, pp. 63–70.

**Books and Reports**

Brown, Lawrence A. *Innovation Diffusion: A New Perspective.* New York: Methuen, 1981.

Buggie, Frederick D. *New Product Development Strategies.* New York: AMACOM, 1981.

Cafarelli, Eugene J. *Developing New Products and Repositioning Mature Brands.* New York: John Wiley and Sons, 1980.

Corbin, R., and Gamache, R. D. *Creating Profitable New Products and Markets.* New York: AMACOM, 1980.

Drucker, Peter F. *Innovation and Entrepreneurship: Practice and Principles.* New York: Harper & Row, 1985.

Hartley, Robert F. *Marketing Mistakes.* Second ed. Columbus: Grid Publishing, 1981.

Hisrich, Robert D., and Peters, Michael P. *Marketing a New Product: Its Planning, Development, and Control.* Menlo Park, Calif.: Benjamin Cummings Publishing, 1978.

————. *Marketing Decisions for New and Mature Products: Planning, Development, and Control.* Columbus: Charles E. Merrill Publishing, 1984.

Hopkins, David S. *New-Product Winners and Losers.* Report no. 773. New York: The Conference Board, 1980.

————. *Options in New-Product Organization.* New York: The Conference Board, 1974.

*International New Product Newsletter.* Boston, Mass.

*The Journal of Product Innovation Management.* New York: Elsevier Science Publications, 1984.

Karger, Delmar W., and Murdick, Robert G. *New Product Venture Management.* New York: Gordon and Breach, 1972.

King, Stephen. *Developing New Brands.* New York: John Wiley and Sons, 1973.

Leroy, George P. *Multinational Product Strategy: A Typology for Analysis of Worldwide Product Innovation and Diffusion.* New York: Praeger, 1976.

*Management of the New Product Function.* New York: Association of National Advertisers, 1980.

Midgley, David F. *Innovation and New Product Marketing.* New York: John Wiley and Sons, 1977.

Nayak, P. Ranganath, and Ketteringham, John M. *Breakthroughs!* New York: Rawson Associates, 1986.

*New Product Management for the 1980s.* New York: Booz, Allen and Hamilton, 1982.

*New Products and Processes.* New York: Newsweek, Inc.

*The New Products Handbook.* Homewood, Ill.: Dow Jones-Irwin, 1986.

*New Products Newletter.* International Intertrade Index.

*New Products—U.S. Department of Commerce U.S. Industrial Outlook.* Washington, D.C.: U.S. Government Printing Office, 1982.

Park, W. R., and Maillie, J. *Strategic Analysis for Venture Evaluation.* Van Nostrand Reinhold, 1982.

Pessemier, Edgar A. *Product Management: Strategy and Organization.* Second ed. New York: John Wiley and Sons, 1982.

*The PIMS Program.* Cambridge, Mass.: The Strategic Planning Institute, 1980.

*Prescription for New Product Success.* New York: American Association of National Advertisers, 1984.

*Preview: New Product Bulletin.* Northbrook, Ill.: A. C. Nielsen Company.

*Product Line Strategies.* Report 816. New York: Conference Board, 1982.

Ray, Michael L. *Creativity in Business.* Garden City: Doubleday, 1986.

Robertson, Thomas S. *Innovative Behavior and Communication.* New York: Holt, Rinehart and Winston, 1971.

Rogers, Everett M. *Bibliography on the Diffusion of Innovations.* East Lansing, Mich.: Department of Communication, Michigan State University, 1971.

————. *Diffusion of Innovations.* New York: Free Press of Glencoe, 1962.

Rogers, Everett M., and Shoemaker, F. Floyd. *Communication of Innovations: A Cross-Cultural Approach.* Second ed. New York: Free Press, 1971.

Rosenau, Milton D., Jr. *Innovation: Managing the Development of Profitable New Products.* Belmont, Calif.: Lifetime Learning Publ., 1982.

Rothberg, R., and Mellot, D. W. *New Product Planning: Management of Marketing/R&D Interface.* Chicago: American Marketing Association, 1977.

Sachs, William S., and Benson, George. *Product Planning and Management.* Tulsa, Okla.: PennWell Books, 1981.

Spitz, A. Edward. *Product Planning.* New York: Petrocelli/Charter, 1977.

Tiegjen, Karl H. *Organizing the Product Planning Function.* New York: AMA, 1963.

Urban, Glen L., and Harser, John R. *Design and Marketing of New Products.* Englewood Cliffs: Prentice-Hall, 1980.

# Index